shaker songs

a musical celebration of peace, harmony, and simplicity

Compiled and edited by Christian Goodwillie
with contributions from Joel Cohen

BLACK DOG
& LEVENTHAL
PUBLISHERS
NEW YORK

Contents

INTRODUCTION

The United Society of Believers in Christ's Second Appearing, commonly called Shakers, is the longest surviving communal religious group in the United States. The Shaker faith—centered around emulating the life and teachings of Christ—was introduced by Mother Ann Lee, whom many Shakers considered to be the first embodiment of the second coming of Christ's church on Earth. This idea is as radical today as it was upon the Shakers' arrival in America in 1774. It was in that year that Mother Ann Lee and eight followers landed in New York, having left their homes in Manchester, England. According to the 1823 manuscript *A Summary View of the Millennial Church*, Ann Lee had endured persecution for her beliefs in her native land and was "directed to repair to America...She received a divine promise that the work of God would greatly increase, and the millennial church would be established in that country." Accordingly, she set out for the new world, making the perilous ocean voyage in order to spread the gospel of Christ's second appearing amid the relative religious freedom of the colonies.

During their first years in America, the lives of the Shakers were not much easier than they had been in England. In 1780, Ann Lee was imprisoned at Albany on charges of treason by a local revolutionary committee. Upon her release she undertook what turned out to be a nearly three-year journey throughout New England and eastern New York, proselytizing to the ripe minds of rural inhabitants. Chief among her doctrines was the idea that humankind could be redeemed from its original sin by confessing to that sin and "taking up the cross" against all things deemed "ungodly," such as anger, prejudice, and lust. This process of conversion would enable a person to return spiritually to the state of grace from which humanity had fallen. By making this choice an individual could "eat of the tree of life and live forever." The reality of accepting Mother's gospel was the effective dissolution of marriages, the sexual relationships associated with them, and the traditional familial roles played by mothers, fathers, and children.

Needless to say, Mother Ann's message was often met with great hostility. Although she converted many, she paid a heavy price for her success, as did her followers. The Shakers, or Believers, as they called themselves, maintained that their testimony and way of life represented "the commencement of that everlasting Kingdom thus seen in prophetic vision." In short, they believed the Millennium, as discussed in the Book of Revelations, was at hand. Because of their exceeding fervor, early Shakers were repeatedly beaten, jailed, and chased out of towns by irate locals who were threatened by the prospect of a loved one joining the sect and renouncing their earthly ties of marriage and family. Mother Ann's death on September 8, 1784—just ten years and one month after her arrival in America—was probably a cumulative result of the abuse and punishment she had endured to spread the Shaker gospel. Nevertheless, her sacrifice was by no means in vain: by 1810, major Shaker communities had been established throughout New England, New York, Ohio, Indiana, and Kentucky.

Over the course of the eighteenth, nineteenth, and twentieth centuries, Shaker communities were established at twenty-five different locations. Some of these communities lasted only a few years, others for 150 years or more, and one community still exists today at Sabbathday Lake, Maine. After the formal organization of the Shaker church by Joseph Meacham in 1787, the Believers came to embrace a communal way of life. The main features of this lifestyle were a confession of sin, the severance of marital and familial relationships and placement into a Shaker family, and the transfer of all personal assets (cash, material goods, property) to the ownership of the community as a whole. A person wishing to join the Shakers would typically make these commitments gradually, dependent on their spiritual growth within the society and the recognition thereof by community leaders.

Over the last 200 years, right up until today, Shaker congregations have been well-springs of remarkable creativity in many branches of human endeavor. These fields have included religion, architecture, agriculture, industry, art, social welfare, education, and music. It is the inimitable Shaker music that forms the focus of this book. Music was a democratic mode of spiritual expression, a blank canvas onto which all individual Believers were welcome to project the feelings and ideas that the Shaker religion had manifested in their hearts. The earliest of these songs was just that, pure wordless feeling. Mother Ann is said to have won over many a convert with her wordless songs.

Shaker worship involved not just music, but also dancing, spinning, and the shaking that inspired outsiders to derisively label believers "Shakers." Eighteenth century accounts of Shaker meetings describe wild scenes of religious enthusiasm. This freedom of movement and expression, which defined the early period of worship, was later formalized into dances of set patterns and motions. Many dance tunes survive, with such illustrative names as "Back Manner," "Turning Shuffle," "March," and "Quick Dance." Most of these songs have no lyrics, but are instead vocalized versions of popular secular fiddle tunes.

New songs were developed as the Shaker missionaries advanced and met with Baptist and Methodist revivalists in the West during the Kentucky Revival, which began in 1800. These hymns, as they came to be known, were instructive in nature, and were intended to elucidate the theological underpinnings of Christ's second appearing for religion-hungry frontier families awaiting salvation. Some of these early hymns were transmitted back to the East, theologically edited, and collected for use in the first Shaker-printed book, *Millennial Praises*, which was made at Hancock, Massachusetts, in 1812 and 1813. The standardized musical presentation of the Shaker gospel made its teachings more accessible to new converts who were still coming to grips with the finer points of Mother's message.

The 1820s and 1830s saw the development of numerous music notation systems by different Shakers, some based on traditional methods and others on original concepts. (For the most complete survey of this process, and of Shaker music in general, see Dr. Daniel Patterson's *The Shaker Spiritual*.) Eventually, the system of small letteral notation was generally accepted as the most efficient and accurate method of notating songs. This system used a central pitch, for instance "c" in the natural major mode, as the focus for a song. The central pitch was placed in the middle of a blank space, or along the center line of a section of lined paper. Pitches were then denoted with letters (for example, "d, e, f, g, a, b, c") placed either above or below the central tonic of "c" to indicate that the note lay in the octave above or below.

This ingenious system allowed people with no formal musical training to read and even write music more easily. The efficiency of the system provided for the quick notation of inspirational songs, which came at the rate of hundreds per year during some particularly ecstatic periods. Elder Henry C. Blinn of Canterbury, New Hampshire, even developed a system for setting Shaker songs into printed letteral notation. His 1852 publication *A Sacred Repository of Anthems and Hymns* is a remarkable record of this achievement. The system of letteral notation was used into the twentieth century by the Shakers, even as they eventually began using traditional music notation.

Up until 1870, instruments were virtually unknown in Shaker music. Certain instruments had been invented by the Shakers, but they were usually for the purposes of demonstrating the principles of music theory. However, as Shaker populations declined in the later nineteenth century, worldly fashions began to creep into the communities, and infiltrated the music as well. The Shakers at Canterbury, New Hampshire, even engaged a local singing master to instruct them in proper vocal technique. Pianos and organs made their way into the villages, and harmonized songs—typical of the Victorian parlor tunes of the day—became the norm. (Prior to this period, harmony was viewed as a special "gift" and was rarely used.) Important printed collections of Shaker music in traditional notation were produced from 1875 all the way until 1908. Because of the Shakers' longstanding commitment to the documentation of their songs, their musical tradition is very much alive and well today. The members of the last Shaker community at Sabbathday Lake, Maine, continue to maintain this musical heritage as an important component of their everyday lives.

There are nearly 1,000 known manuscript songbooks that contain the collective creative and spiritual energy of the many who have embraced Shakerism since its arrival in America in 1774. This rich heritage is as of yet largely untapped and will undoubtedly still yield musical treasures on par with the well known Shaker song "Simple Gifts." It is important to remember that these songs are a record of intensely religious personal experiences. To twenty-first-century readers, the lyrics or circumstances of the songs' reception may seem whimsical, naïve, or strange. However, at their core lies deep belief, a belief so strong that whole lives were dedicated to carrying out its principles. Perhaps this small collection will serve to further some of the messages of love and equality so important to the Shakers then and now.

Christian Goodwillie, June 2002

MOTHER ANN'S SONG

Ann Lee was born in Manchester, England, in either late February or early March of 1736. (For a full discussion of the controversy surrounding her birth date see the song "A HYMN COMPOSED On the Centennial birthday of Mother Ann Lee March 1st, 1837".) Her father, John Lees (Ann later dropped the final "s" of her last name), was a blacksmith by trade; her mother's name is unknown. Ann was the second oldest of eight children. The family lived in cramped quarters on Toad Lane. According to the 1816 edition of *Testimonies...of Our Blessed Mother Ann Lee*, early in life Ann developed "a great abhorrence of the fleshly cohabitation of the sexes...she often admonished her mother against it."

In 1758 she began attending the worship services of a small religious sect called the Wardley Society. This sect, named for its founders John and Jane Wardley, met in private homes in the Manchester suburb of Bolton. In the Wardley Society, Ann

Above: A detail showing Mother Ann from An Emblem of the Heavenly Sphere, *drawn by Polly Collins at Hancock, Massachusetts, in 1854.*

found people sympathetic to her strong religious impulses, as well as her belief in sexual abstinence.

Ann was married to blacksmith Abraham Standerin (his last name is variously given as Standley or Stanley) in 1762. The couple had four children, none of whom survived infancy. During these years Ann was afflicted with "such severe sufferings, [that] for six weeks together her [body] was so reduced that she was as weak as an infant, and was fed and supported by others." In 1770, Ann received revelations regarding "the root and foundation of human depravity; and of the very transgression of the first man and woman, in the garden of Eden." Subsequently she "bore an open testimony against the lustful gratifications of the flesh," and was "received and acknowledged as the first spiritual Mother in Christ, and the second heir of the covenant of life in the new creation." From that point on the Wardley Society called her "Mother," and her life's mission had begun.

Mother Ann's Song

Bow low, low, low and cry to God, Dear chil - dren,

with your Mo - ther. For I do weep, Yea

weep and mourn, I weep for my dear chil - dren.

TRUMPET OF PEACE

Shaker tradition has it that Mother Ann and eight followers left Liverpool, England, on May 19, 1774. The story of their voyage was mythologized in *A Summary View of the Millennial Church*, published by the Shakers in 1823.

While on their passage, they went forth, in obedience of their inward feelings, to praise God in songs and dances. This offended the captain to such a degree, that he threatened to throw them overboard, if they attempted the like exercise again....But that God in whom they trusted...had power to protect them. This he did in a marvelous manner. It was in the evening, in time of a storm; and the ship suddenly sprung a leak, occasioned by the starting of a plank between wind and water. The water now flowed in so rapidly...that the whole ship's crew were greatly alarmed....But Mother Ann maintained her confidence in God, and said, "Captain, be of good cheer; there shall not be a hair of our heads perish; we shall arrive safely in America. I just now saw two bright angels of God standing by the mast, through whom I received the promise."...Shortly after this, a large wave struck the ship with great violence, and the loose plank was instantly closed into place.

Above: A detail depicting "The Savior's Ship of Safety" from Miranda Barber's 1848 drawing
From Holy Mother Wisdom...To Eldress Dana or Mother.

Trumpet of Peace

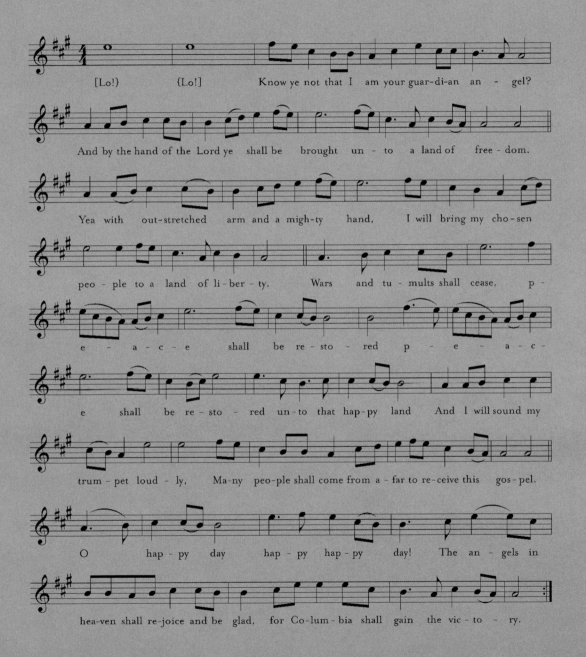

[Lo!} {Lo!] Know ye not that I am your guar-di-an an - gel?

And by the hand of the Lord ye shall be brought un - to a land of free - dom.

Yea with out-stretched arm and a migh-ty hand, I will bring my cho-sen

peo - ple to a land of li-ber - ty. Wars and tu - mults shall cease, p -

e - a - c - e shall be re-sto - red p - e - a-c-

e shall be re-sto - red un-to that hap-py land And I will sound my

trum - pet loud - ly, Ma-ny peo-ple shall come from a - far to re-ceive this gos-pel.

O hap - py day hap - py hap-py day! The an - gels in

hea-ven shall re-joice and be glad, for Co-lum - bia shall gain the vic - to - ry.

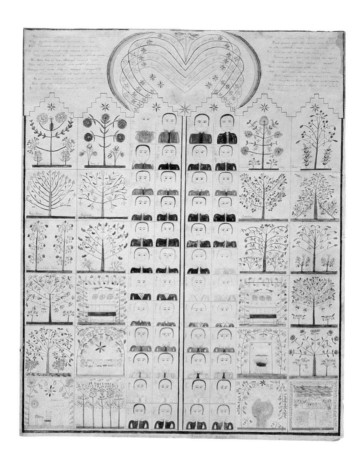

SOLEMN SONG
OF THE ANCIENTS

The mystical, wordless "Solemn Songs" are among the oldest in the Shaker repertoire. They were copied down years later by Shaker scribes, from oral tradition. This one, like others of the genre, seems to be in a rather free and rhapsodic style, more difficult to notate accurately within the Shaker system than the measured pieces that

Above: Polly Collins's 1854 drawing An Emblem of the Heavenly Sphere *depicts "the world above where saints in order, are combined in love."*

form the majority of the repertoire. According to the Sabbathday Lake Shakers, "Elder Otis Sawyer of the Maine Ministry copied this song preserved from the time of the First Parents while on a visit to New Lebanon in 1842." These visitations were instrumental in expanding the breadth of the Shaker music canon, as they offered opportunities for communities to share music with one another.

Solemn Song of the Ancients

(some rhythms conjectural)

STONE PRISON

Mother Ann Lee was persecuted and jailed for her beliefs and missionary preaching, both in England and America. A number of beautiful Shaker songs refer to the tribulations she and the other early Shakers underwent. The manuscript annotation to this one reads: "This song Mother Ann sang through an Inst[rument] at the table when the Family was eating bread and water. Harvard [Massachusetts] 1842."

This song recalls the imprisonment of Mother Ann in England. During the revival known as Mother's Work (circa 1837–1847), Believers began to celebrate Mother Ann's birthday (February 29th) as well as the arrival of the First Shakers (August 6th). It was during such a time that the community had gathered to remember the sufferings of Mother Ann while in prison for the sake of the Gospel.

—The Shakers of Sabbathday Lake

Stone Prison

1. How can I but love my dear faith-ful chil - dren, Who're wil - ling to bear and suf - fer with me. When I was on earth and in a cold pri - son I cry'd to my God to re-mem-ber poor me.

2. I pray-ed to God to pro-tect my dear chil - dren, to strength-en the weak and com - fort the strong. For I was dis - tressed and in a stone pri - son, And none but my God to pro-tect me from harm.

Above: A 1794 drawing of the courthouse and prison at Albany where Mother Ann was tried and jailed.

Rights of Conscience

Rights of con-science in these days, Now de-mand our sol-emn praise;

Here we see what God has done, By his ser - vant

Wash - ing - ton, Who with wis - dom was en - dow'd

By an an - gel, thru the cloud, And led forth in

Wis - dom's plan, To se - cure the rights of man.

"Arm yourselves, unsheath the sword!
(Cries the servant of the Lord,)
Rights of freedom we'll maintain,
and our independence gain."
Fleets and armies he withstood,
In the strength of Jehu's God;
Proud Cornwallis and Burgoyne,
With their armies soon resign.

Thus the valiant conqu'ror stood
To defend his country's good,
Till a treaty he confirms,
Settling peace on his own terms.
Having clos'd these warlike scenes,
Chosen men he then convenes;
These a constitution plan'd,
To protect this ransom'd land.

Cyrus-like, was Washington
Call'd to do what he has done;
We his noble acts record,
Tho' he did not know the Lord:
As a prudent man of blood,
He the hosts of earth withstood;
Nature's rights he did restore,
God from him requir'd no more.

Mighty Christians, stout and bold!
Full of lust as you can hold,
Fighting for religious rights!
God has notic'd all such fights:
Still your souls are not releas'd,
Bound by sin and wicked priests;
Tho' your country has been sav'd,
You in bondage are enslav'd.

With all this you're not content,
Still on bondage you are bent,
Binding the poor negro too,
He must be a slave to you!
Yet of Washington you boast,
Spread his fame thro, every coast,
Bury him with great ado,
Precepts and examples too!

Did you think in seventy five,
When the states were all alive,
When they did for freedom sue,
God was deaf and blind like you?

You were fighting on one side,
To build up your lust and pride;
God was bringing in a plan,
To defeat the pride of man.

Liberty is but a sound,
If the conscience still is bound;
Could you but her reigns control,
You would creed-bind every soul.
You, and when we say 'tis you,
We've no respect to Greek or Jew;
But boldly tell you what we mean,
Your vile Church that lives in sin.

Now we mean to let you know,
We've not treated freedom so;
Since God's Kingdom has come in,
We find freedom from all sin.
O, ye priest-bound souls, come out!
Help us raise the living shout;
Never heed your former stuff,
You have prov'd it long enough.

See the woman's seed advance,
Glor'ous in Emmanuel's dance!
At this strange victor'ous play,
Earth and heavens flee away:
Swift as light'ning see them move,
Labouring in unfeigned love:
God, thro' Mother we adore,
Hate the flesh and sin no more.

HOLY ORDER SONG

It was one of the founding Shakers, Father Joseph Meacham, who introduced the Holy Order dance in 1787 or 1788. "I received this manner of worship by the 'Revelation of God' & it must be handed down to you from generation to generation," he said. It was still being danced in Sabbathday Lake as late as 1868. This is one of many melodies that served for the Holy Order.

The Holy Order was among the first dance steps introduced by Father Joseph Meacham in the 1780s. It was the longest-lived of all the dances, being used for nearly a century. This song was received by Elder Otis [Sawyer] from the spirit of "Elder Brother Oliver Holmes," who had recently passed to the spirit land.

—The Shakers at Sabbathday Lake

Holy Order Song

The Holy Laws of Zion.

The Lord announces Himself in His true Character & Power.

Thus saith the Lord; I am the Word; I am the Law; I am the Beginning and the Ending; I am that I AM, the Holy One of Israel. Before ME there was not, and above ME there is none; but your Eternal Mother, Wisdom, is ever by my side, and her Glory is my Delight, and my Delight her Glory.

And to all who faithfully keep our commandments, our laws and our statutes, WE have, from the foundation of the world, and will, to the end of time, make ourselves known in truth to them, and clearly show to them the path of their duty, through such means as we may chuse. And let no one plead for indulgence in Zion, nor seek to evade the cross which I have for them, saith the Lord; which ^cross they must faithfully bear, or never enter my Kingdom. And they that turn their sense to look to Sodoma var sin, shall be like unto righteous Lot's Vas farane, upon whom my wrath and judg-

ment

Above: A manuscript page from **Millennial Laws**, *first instituted by Mother Lucy Wright at New Lebanon, New York, in 1821.*

REVIVAL SONG

Elder Benjamin Seth Youngs, one of the three Shaker Brethren who made the missionary journey to the West from New Lebanon, New York, in 1805, remained in Kentucky until his death in 1855 at the age of eighty-one. Youngs was the chief author of *The Testimony of Christ's Second Appearing* (1808), which was the first large scale attempt to present and explain Shaker beliefs. Youngs was also an Elder at the South

Above: The Whirling Gift, *as depicted in the 1848 book by Shaker apostate David Lamson,* Two Years' Experience Among the Shakers.

Union, Kentucky, community. His earliest journal, now known as *South Union Journal A*, recorded the formative years of Shakerism in the West. "Revival Song" was notated in a later copy of the journal with the following description: "June 1815 Sabbath 11th Public Meeting was free & unrestrained. The feeling & spirit was such as to remove all restraints. The presence of the world being no obstacle [a reference to non-Shaker, or worldly, spectators at the service]. They sang the well known song Revival Song. The above was sung, round after round, mid shaking rejoicing stamping & turning, the sound was as if thunder & quaking, or breath of fire— so affecting it was that many spectators shed tears." Scenes like this one were a powerful factor in converting people to Shakerism.

Revival Song

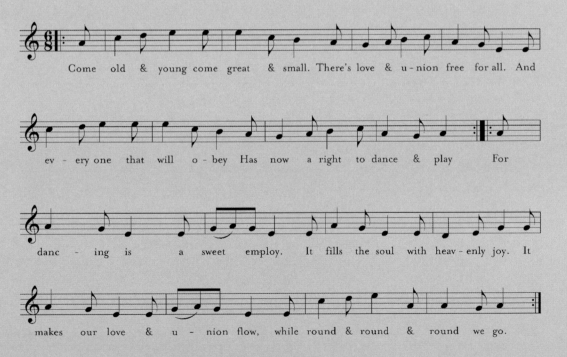

Come old & young come great & small. There's love & u-nion free for all. And
ev-ery one that will o-bey Has now a right to dance & play For
danc - ing is a sweet employ. It fills the soul with heav-enly joy. It
makes our love & u - nion flow, while round & round & round we go.

THE TESTIMONY OF ETERNAL TRUTH

This hymn is the introductory song in the first Shaker-printed book, the 1812 hymnal *Millennial Praises*. In 1805 three Shaker brethren were sent west from New Lebanon (later Mt. Lebanon), New York, to investigate the religious fervor then occurring in Kentucky. The Kentucky Revival, as it came to be known, was a massive religious awakening during which rival Protestant sects battled for converts.

The Shaker Brethren were relatively successful in their efforts to spread Mother Ann's word. Shaker missionary work in the West resulted in the establishment of communities at South Union and Pleasant Hill, Kentucky, and Union Village and Watervliet, Ohio. One of the key musical developments to come out of the Shaker experience in the West was the large number of hymns intended to elucidate the major tenets of the Shaker faith. Many of these hymns, including "The Testimony of Eternal Truth," are attributed to Richard McNemar, an early convert from Turtle Creek, Ohio. McNemar's importance to the Shaker mission in the West cannot be overstated. He wrote many of the hymns in *Millennial Praises*, as well as a narrative entitled *The Kentucky Revival* (1807), which provides an excellent eyewitness account of the bizarre events then taking place in Kentucky. "Testimony" clearly explains the Shaker belief in a God whose duality encompasses the male aspect of the Father, and the female aspect, Wisdom. It denounces the idea of the triune Christ, instead arguing for the "two in one"—the male and female attributes of the Christ spirit. These ideas are just as radical today as they were in 1812.

Right: The title page to the 1808 edition of Richard McNemar's colorful firsthand account of the Kentucky Revival.

THE

KENTUCKY REVIVAL,

OR,

A SHORT HISTORY

OF THE LATE EXTRAORDINARY OUT-POURING OF THE
SPIRIT OF GOD, IN THE WESTERN STATES OF
AMERICA, AGREEABLY TO SCRIPTURE-
PROMISES, AND PROPHECIES CON-
CERNING THE LATTER DAY:

WITH A BRIEF ACCOUNT

OF THE ENTRANCE AND PROGRESS OF WHAT
THE WORLD CALL

SHAKERISM,

AMONG THE SUBJECTS OF THE LATE REVIVAL
IN *OHIO* AND *KENTUCKY.*

PRESENTED TO THE
TRUE ZION-TRAVELLER,
AS A MEMORIAL OF THE WILDERNESS JOURNEY.

―――――――――

BY RICHARD M'NEMAR.

―――――――――

" When ye see a cloud rise out of the west, straightway ye say,
" there cometh a shower; and so it is: And when YE FEEL
" the south wind blow, ye say, there will be heat; and it
" cometh to pass—Can ye not discern the signs of the times."
CHRIST.

―――――――――

CINCINNATI—PRINTED:
ALBANY; RE-PRINTED BY E. AND E. HOSFORD.

1808.

The Testimony of Eternal Truth

"Tune by Lydia Comstock, En., Ch., in or about the year 1811."

God of sal - va - tion, pow'r and grace, Un -
known to man's a - pos - tate race, Thy glo - ry,
veil'd with - in a cloud, E - ludes the search - es
of the proud. Thy na - ture and e - ter - nal
law, The wis - est mor - tal nev - er
saw; Nor can thy works be tru - ly seen, But
by the soul that's pure and clean.

Now from a carnal nature freed,
Thy everlasting name we read;
And love that full parental name,
From which our living spirits came.
Long ere this fleeting world began,
Or dust was fashion'd into man,
There Power and Wisdom we can view,
Names of the Everlasting Two.

The Father's high eternal throne
Was never fill'd by one alone:
There Wisdom holds the Mother's seat,
And is the Father's helper-meet.
This vast creation was not made
Without the fruitful Mother's aid;
For by the works of god we know
The fountain-head from which they flow.

"Let us make man" was rightly said,
And in God's image Man was made,
One flesh and blood, two in one name,
Both naked, yet no cause of shame.
While in one form alone he stood,
His maker saw il was not good;
Nor could his order be complete,
Until he found an helper-meet.

To be as gods, before the time,
    Was man's temptation, and his crime:
While in his weak and infant state,
    It was not for him to create:
But tempted by a pois'nous brute,
He took of this forbiden fruit,
And cleaving to his kindred dust,
Became a slave to his own lust.

Now on inferior pleasures bent,
    His soul forgets its true descent:
But though vain man became a beast,
    The law of nature never ceas'd:
By male and female join'd in one,
The old creation still goes on;
But sure they must be born again,
Or linger in eternal pain.

When the old world of flesh and blood,
Was swept away by Noah's flood,
The ark preserv'd a chosen few,
To typify what Christ would do.
But circumcision first reveal'd
The seat where lust had been conceal'd,
And in the flesh of the foreskin,
Was found the root of ev'ry sin.

The monstrous beast, and bloody whore
Riegn'd thirteen hundred years and more;
And under foot the truth was trod,
By their mysterious three-fold God:
But while they placed in the He
Their sacred co-eternal Three,
A righteous persecuted few
Ador'd the everlasting Two.

The Holy Ghost at length did bear
Th' anointed one, the second heir,
A virgin soul, a holy child,
A Mother pure and undefil'd:
In her the heirship is complete,
In her the types and figures meet,
And God's last building stands upon
The sacred truth of two in one.

THE TREE OF LIFE

This early hymn appears in the 1812 collection *Millennial Praises*, printed at Hancock, Massachusetts, by Josiah Tallcott, Jr. The poem is attributed to Richard McNemar, the chief hymnodist among the early western Shakers. The tree is symbolic of the respite to be found in the confession of sin. Confession, a prerequisite for someone joining the Shaker church, was the key, for as the lyrics state, the tree is "not seen by sinners [sic] eyes." Those who confess may partake of its fruit, which their "wounded souls did heal." The continuing challenge of Shaker life was to "bear the cross," meaning the commitment of celibacy and steadfast devotion to the work and worship of Shaker life. This hymn promises that those who "bear the cross from day to day" will "find that fruit in its pure state, and eat and live forever."

Above: Hannah Cohoon's The Tree of Life, *drawn at Hancock, Massachusetts,*
in 1854, is perhaps the best known Shaker image.

The Tree of Life

Largo

On Zi - on's hill is clear - ly seen, By

souls who do not live un - clean, The

tree of life, for - ev - er green, Of God the

Fa - ther's plant - - ing: Est - a - blish'd by the

Lord's comm - and, This tree will there for - ev - er

stand, Diff - us - ing bless - ings thru the land, Of

Christ the Sav - iour's grant - - ing.

THE MIDNIGHT CRY

This early hymn is mentioned at least twice in Shaker journals. The first mention appears in a Kentucky-Revival era journal from South Union, which recounts a camp meeting near convert Matthew Houston's house in Paint Lick, Kentucky. "Sabbath, May 25, 1806. In the woods near Matthews from 80 to 800 people assembled—Benj. [Benjamin Seth Youngs] spoke 3 hours, standing on a log and the people sat on rails— He discoursed on salvation from all sin...After this we sang the Hymn entitled the Midnight Cry."

Above: An illustration of evening meeting at Mt. Lebanon, New York, from The Graphic, *May 14, 1870.*

"The Midnight Cry" also appears in the reminiscences of Rhoda Blake, an early convert from Savoy in northwestern Massachusetts. She recorded the events of Autumn 1816 as follows: "One time the Elders came over...and Calvin [Green] was to speak to the people, and try to open their understanding and put down their hatred and persecution...While the company were singing their first piece, the ruffs opened the door and insulted them by shooting saccarine [sic] matter into their laps. They were singing The Midnight Cry."

The Midnight Cry

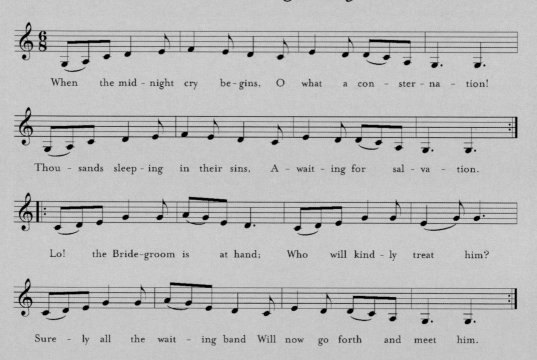

When the mid - night cry be - gins, O what a con - ster - na - tion!

Thou - sands sleep - ing in their sins, A - wait - ing for sal - va - tion.

Lo! the Bride-groom is at hand; Who will kind - ly treat him?

Sure - ly all the wait - ing band Will now go forth and meet him.

UNTITLED DANCE TUNE

The following account of Shaker worship was written down by Moses Guest, who had visited the Watervliet, New York, Shaker community on Sunday, October 10, 1796:

I beheld 24 men dancing at one end of the room, and 20 women at the other. They …were formed four deep. They kept good time, though frequently trembled as if much convulsed—this they call the working of the spirit. After continuing in this way for about an hour and a half…they all retired to a house…where they partook of some refreshment; but soon commenced singing a kind of gibberish, which they call an unknown tongue. After about an hour's intermission they assembled again and formed two deep; they then all sang in their unknown tongue, appearing, at times, to be very much convulsed; after a continued dancing and trembling for half an hour, they ceased singing, and after many heavy sighs and groans, and much twisting and trembling, one of their elders, in broken accents, muttered out, let us, my dear friends, endeavour to praise God in the dance…in this way they continued about an hour, appearing, at times, very much agitated.

Above: This blue shoe is of the type that the Sisters would have worn to meeting in the 1850s, though its style is that of a shoe from the late eighteenth century.

Untitled Dance Tune

Spiritual Wine

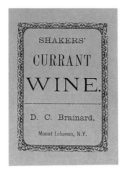  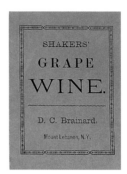

This lively song is attributed in different manuscripts to either Brother Issachar Bates or Brother Richard McNemar. The manuscript from which this version derives states that it was "Learned of Eldress Cassandana Goodrich, in the year 1811." Eldress, or Mother, Dana presided as First Eldress of the Hancock Bishopric Ministry from 1796 until 1848.

"Spiritual Wine" appears in the collection *Millennial Praises*, first printed at Hancock in 1812. The lyrics describe how tasting the "wine" of Shakerism causes one to "stagger and reel," and to "break forth into songs, To express how delightful they feel." Accepting the Shaker faith was so intoxicating that the author declares, "I want no other bliss, And I care not much how the world goes."

The Shakers' attitude towards alcohol changed periodically over the course of the nineteenth century. Early in the century they were frequently accused of drinking to excess, and of calling rum "The spirit of God." These accusations were likely unfounded, though the Shakers did produce and use alcohol. Whiskey was distilled in the Kentucky communities, and blackberry, cherry, elderberry, grape, currant, red currant, and apple wines were made at Mt. Lebanon, New York. However, by the mid 1880s, Elder Frederick Evans of the North Family of Mt. Lebanon preached total abstinence from alcohol, maintaining that it "dethroned" reason.

Spiritual Wine

"Composed by Richard McNemar, U.V.
Learned of Eldress Cassandana Goodrich,
in the year 1811."

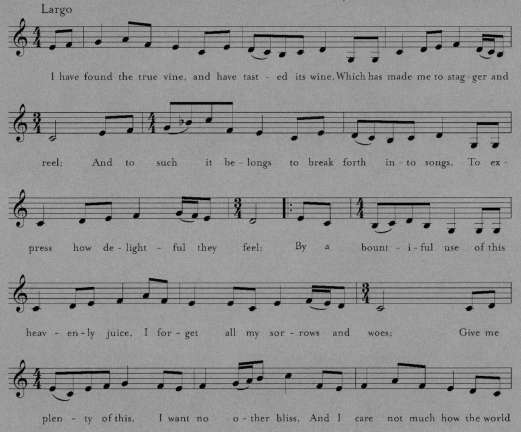

Largo

I have found the true vine, and have tast - ed its wine, Which has made me to stag-ger and

reel; And to such it be - longs to break forth in - to songs, To ex -

press how de - light - ful they feel; By a bount - i - ful use of this

heav - en - ly juice, I for - get all my sor - rows and woes; Give me

plen - ty of this, I want no o - ther bliss, And I care not much how the world

goes, goes, goes, And I care not much how the world goes.

Left: Labels from some of the fruit wines produced for sale at Mt. Lebanon, New York.

INDUSTRY

This light-hearted tune celebrates the Shaker work ethic by comparing it with industrious animals and insects. Life was vastly more difficult in the eighteenth and nineteenth centuries than it is today. The Shakers approached the colossal workload necessary to maintain their large communities with an outlook that was exceptional even then. One of Mother Ann's sayings states, "Do all your work as if you had a thousand years to live, and as you would if you knew you must die tomorrow." This statement is reflective of the way in which the Shakers sought to remove themselves from earthly time. After all, if the Millennium had truly commenced, then it was their duty to build heaven on Earth and make a seamless transition to eternal reward.

All labor was sacred among the Shakers, and each task was to be completed with the

Above: Sisters from Enfield, Connecticut, with dairying equipment.

utmost care and attention to quality. This was necessary because each person was dependent on every other, and all had to work to the best of their ability. As the lyrics to this song reveal, "I for one feel much inclined to work for one & all And when I loose this liberal mind I shall not work at all....I'll settle down in black despair and own I'm not of God."

Industry

"Alonzo Hollister, MtL Chh 1849 I.B."

All na - ture calls for bu - sy hands For this is Hea -

ven's de - cree The beasts, the birds, the in - sects stand A mon -

i - tor for me The lit - tle bu - sy art - ful bee

Works ev - ery shi - ning hour And her in - dus - try

I can see in every open - ing flow - er

37

THE HARVEST

The Shakers are renowned for having pioneered the packaging of garden seeds for sale. The communities of the Hancock Bishopric—Hancock and Tyringham, Massachusetts, and Enfield, Connecticut—were among the greatest producers of garden seeds. Enfield began producing seeds in great quantities in 1802, with Hancock and Tyringham following shortly thereafter. By 1819 the Hancock Shakers had signed an agreement with some of the New York communities whereby all would sell only top quality seeds grown at the communities. The Shakers recognized that a good business reputation necessitated a quality product.

At Hancock the seed harvest began in June with the first salsify seeds, and then cole

Above: Brother Levi Shaw of the North Family at Mt. Lebanon, New York.

and root vegetables in July and August. Bean, cucumber, corn, and squash seeds were harvested in September. The last crops to come in were tomatoes, peppers, pumpkins, and asparagus in October. Hancock seed salesmen worked routes extending well into the Midwest by the 1830s, while Enfield shipped seeds by water to Southern markets. Onion and watermelon seeds were among the most popular varieties grown in the Bishopric. Seed packets were printed, cut, and pasted by hand. Once filled, these packets were placed into wooden Shaker seed boxes, which were then taken to country stores by Brethren on their seed selling routes. "Seed Lists" were used by merchants to place their orders with the Shakers. In the fall, unsold seeds were collected, accounts settled, and orders taken for the following year.

The Harvest

Our sup-port we'll ga - ther in, For the har - vest time is come.

Now to reap we will be-gin. Will you all now help us on?

'Twas by Christ the seed was sown, Now the har - vest does ap - pear;

Now the crops are ful - ly grown. Reap, o reap, get e - ver - y spear.

A QUICK SONG

Ecstatic movement was the way in which the first Shakers expressed themselves in worship. These movements could be any number of things, from jerking the body violently, to pounding the floor, whirling in place, or even shoving fellow worshipers. Following Mother Ann's death and the formal organization of the church by Father Joseph Meacham, new dances were instituted. These dances were planned out, and served to regularize the Shaker meeting.

"A Quick Song" would have been sung to accompany a dance performed in a circular manner. Shaker music scholar Dr. Daniel Patterson has reconstructed the

Above: An engraving depicting Shaker meeting at New Lebanon, New York, circa 1830. The top hat and seated woman in the foreground presumably signify that "worldly" visitors were observing the meeting.

dance as follows: "…the vocal band [singers who did not dance] stood in two rows in the center of the room. Around them the worshipers, two by two, formed a large circle. The men made up one half and the women the other. For the first section of the tune they skipped around the room. In the last two beats of the section they turned toward the center, striking into the single shuffle for the remainder of the tune." In the nineteenth century great crowds of spectators would gather to watch the Shakers perform their elaborate dances. While the public was usually welcome at meetings, they too were divided according to sex on either side of the room.

A Quick Song

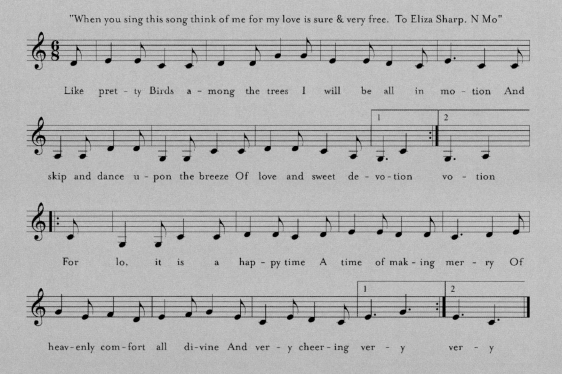

"When you sing this song think of me for my love is sure & very free. To Eliza Sharp. N Mo"

Like pret - ty Birds a - mong the trees I will be all in mo - tion And

skip and dance u - pon the breeze Of love and sweet de - vo - tion vo - tion

For lo, it is a hap - py time A time of mak - ing mer - ry Of

heav - enly com - fort all di - vine And ver - y cheer - ing ver - y ver - y

A HYMN COMPOSED ON THE CENTENNIAL BIRTHDAY OF MOTHER ANN LEE MARCH 1ST 1837

Mother Ann Lee's actual date of birth has been a matter of some confusion for more than two hundred years. The 1816 edition of *Testimonies of the Life, Character, Revelations and Doctrines of Our Ever Blessed Mother Ann Lee* states that she was born in 1736: "It is said that she was born on the 28th day of February; but the fact is not fully ascertained. It is, however, probable that she was born near that time." The following hymn asserts that she was born on March 1st, 1737. However, her birthday is most commonly given as February 29, 1736, a mystical day that occurs only once every four years. Born to John Lees and his wife at Toad Lane in Manchester, England, Ann later dropped the final "s" and became Ann Lee. The hymn celebrates Ann Lee's eventual voyage to America, that "peaceful land where freedom's holy ark shall stand."

Above: Mother Ann's gravestone in the Shaker cemetery at Watervliet, New York.

A HYMN COMPOSED On the Centennial birthday of Mother Ann Lee March 1st 1837

O ha-il the bright au-spi-cious morn When our blest

Mo-ther Ann was born In whom hath God the

light dis-played For which ten thou-sands long have prayed

From frown-ing Eng-land's boast-ful seat Be-hold her

gen-tle band re-treat Thro stor-my seas and

dan-ger dri-ven Their trust their guide the God of hea-ven.

SONG OF COLOVIN

Birds were regular visitors to the Shakers during the Era of Manifestations. They appear repeatedly in many different guises in gift drawings of the time. Sometimes they are "Heavenly Comforters," or "a dove of Peace," or "A Dove of Purity," and other times they are bearers of heavenly objects or rewards. From numerous drawings it would seem that Mother Ann repeatedly sent "her little dove" as a messenger of encouragement and approval to her children on earth. One gift drawing depicts a "Wreath brought by Mother's little dove," which contained "Mother's love." Even the Savior had his own dove. Birds were also frequently the bearers of songs whose lyrics are presumably a bird language of some sort. "Song of Colovin," recorded by Mary Hazard, is remarkable for its strange rhythms and even stranger lyrics. One wonders what "Elder Sister & Betsy" made of this bizarre little performance.

Song of Colovin

Sung by a little bird of Paradise (Colovin by name) that come to see its mate, which was sent to Elder Sister & Betsy, with a song some days before. Learned...Oct 8th 1839

Above: **Dove with rings,** *attributed to an unknown artist from Mt. Lebanon, New York.*

CALL FOR LOVE

This song was sent to Joanna Kitchell at New Lebanon, New York, by Mother Lucy on September 9, 1839. By that time, the revival now known as the Era of Manifestations, or Mother's Work, had gained considerable momentum since its advent the previous August. Spirit visitations at meeting were a common occurrence, with inspired songs and sermons being regularly delivered through Shaker instruments. "Call for Love" is of particular interest, as the manuscript calls for the singers to "Shout" for extended periods on fixed pitches. Such specific instructions were certainly not unusual for the Era of Manifestations, but are not often found in manuscripts written before that time.

Joanna Kitchell was born on July 4, 1796, and was admitted to the Union Village, Ohio, Shaker community in 1807. She joined the New Lebanon community in 1812. In 1840 her occupation was listed as a "weaver of tape," presumably for chairs. She became Farm Deaconess in 1858, managing the agricultural business of one of the New Lebanon Shaker families. She died on May 25, 1878.

A singing meeting, as depicted in the December 1885, issue of Frank Leslie's Popular Monthly.

Call For Love

O breth-ren and sis-ters re-joice O re-joice for I have love , yea Moth-er's heav' -nly love for you

O I do love my bless-ed Moth-er, and I know my

Moth-er does love me. And I will re-joice in Moth-er's love love, It is flow-ing

free and pure I do love my Moth-er's love love, It is a safe-guard firm and sure.

BLESSING AND LOVE

This gift song is from the early days of the Era of Manifestations, or Mother's Work, an intense period of religious revival among the Shakers. Mother's Work began at the South Family in Watervliet, New York, in 1837. Although prophetic visions and religious enthusiasm had always been a part of Shaker life, 1837 saw the advent of what was to become the most intensely creative period in the sect's history.

Sarah Ann Standish was a Sister at Mt. Lebanon. Born in Rochester, Massachusetts, in 1809, she was admitted to the North Family at Mt. Lebanon, New York, in 1831. She was 30 years old when she received this song from Mother Ann. Seven years later she was to receive the drawing at right from Holy Mother Wisdom. During her life Sister Sarah was variously employed making bonnets and soap, braiding whips, and nursing sick Believers. She died in 1895 at the age of 84.

Right: From Holy Mother Wisdom to Sarah Ann Standish, *drawn by Sarah Bates,
Miranda Barber, and Polly Reed in 1847 at Mt. Lebanon, New York.*

Blessing and Love

"Sent from Mother Ann
to Sarah Ann Standish.
October 4th 1840."

O O re - joice my faith - ful si lo ve ne re - joice

and be glad for sure - ly I love thee. Yea the bles-sings of the

hea ven — ly hosts are yours. So So march ye on march march

march on, till ye en - ter the k - i - n - g - d - o - m of hea - ven,

where all faith - ful souls do re-joice in the God of their sal - va - tion

Press on press on for this king - dom, the prize of sal -

va - tion, The vic - to - ry is yours Then you can shout ho - ly

praises to the Lord, for-ev-er more   So   So bee - n-e - n-

c-o-u-r - a-g-e-d my pre - et-ty   pre-ty pre-ty c-h-i-l - d

Re - Re-j   o - i - c - - e   in my sweet-est love love

ANGEL INVITATION

This song expresses the Shaker belief that one is capable of living without sin, as first demonstrated by Jesus Christ, and later by Mother Ann. Confession, a cornerstone of conversion to Shakerism, allowed an individual to break cleanly with the past and "Leave all sin behind." Once so freed, one could "Seek and find the gifts of God" through Shaker life and worship.

Above: Wreath brought by Mother's little dove, *drawn by Polly Collins*
in 1853 at Hancock, Massachusetts.

Angel Invitation

1. Come a-long my Chil-dren dear Leave all sin be-hind you,
2. They will lead you safe-ly on To the land of free-dom,
3. O that is a bet-ter land, Its glo-ries how en-ti-cing,
4. Leave be-hind all earth-ly things Come and be pro-gres-sing,

Ga-ther to my Or-der near An-gels there can find you.
Where the faith-ful all ap-pear In true love and beau-ty.
On its bor-ders An-gels stand Ear-nest-ly in-vi-ting.
Seek and find the gifts of God, They are worth pos-ses-sing.

(Lo-dle lo-dle lo-dle lo lo-dle lo-dle lo lo

lo-dle lo-dle lo-dle lo lo-dle lo-dle lo lo)

53

CHRISTOPHER COLUMBUS'S MARCH

The spirits of many important historical figures visited Shaker communities during the Era of Manifestations. No less a personage than Christopher Columbus sent this tune to Augustus Blase of Watervliet, New York, on August 25, 1840. The lyrics use maritime metaphors to make the comparison between Columbus's voyage of discovery and the committed Believer's lifelong voyage of spiritual discovery. Columbus addresses each individual Shaker as "my lovely companion," furthering the idea that they are explorers like himself. Travelers on both journeys brave the unknown, yet like Columbus, the faithful Believer "shall safe embark, On Canaan's happy shore." The lyric describing the "rolling seas of time" is particularly poignant in its evocation of life's uncertainty, whether one lives within the faith or without.

Above: A detail depicting Christopher Columbus taken from An Emblem of the Heavenly Sphere *by Polly Collins, drawn at Hancock, Massachusetts, in 1854.*

Christopher Columbus's March

"Sent from Christopher Columbus to Augustus Blase of Watervliet, August 25th 1840."

O my love - ly com - pan - ion, wilt thou, wilt thou,

b - r - a - v - e all dan - gers while cross - ing o'er the t - e - m - p - e - s - t - u -

o - u - s s - e - - a, the roll - ing sea of

time. And wilt thou ev - er faith - ful be. O yea, O yea,

Y - E - A Then you shall safe em - bark, On Ca - naan's

hap - py shore, Re - joic - ing in the Lord, For - ev - er ev - er more

more Yea we will sing a joy - ful song, O ho -

ly Ju - bi - lee, And we will raise a joy - ful

ANGEL OF LOVE

Born in Manchester, England, in 1811, Eliza Ann Taylor arrived at New Lebanon, New York, with her family in 1819. By 1844 she had become Eldress of the Church Family. In 1856 she was appointed assistant to Eldress Betsey Bates in the Central Ministry. Sister Eliza attained the highest female rank within the Shaker church in 1869, that of First Eldress, a position she held until her death in 1891. Her importance within the community is evidenced by the fact that Mother Ann sent her the following song, and Mother Lucy (Mother Ann's successor) sent the drawing opposite through medium Polly Jane Reed at Mt. Lebanon, New York, in 1849.

Angel of Love

O I am an

An-gel of love, I come from the ci-ty of love, And I have brought on my wings ho-ly and pure

love, Ho-ly and pure love, ho — ly and pure love, From our bless-ed Sav - iour and

ho - ly Mo - ther So re-joice in this love, My won sa na ve, My won-sa-na ka-ren-e

le ren O

come come a - way from the von a von e val of this world and re-joice with me

Pret - ty love, pret - ty love, Mo-thers love is free

Left: A present from Mother Lucy to Eliza Ann Taylor *prophesies Taylor's future leadership role in the lines: "my ministering Angels shall gather many souls, whom I shall call upon thee to feed and clothe...You shall be their Shepherd & they shall be my people saith WISDOM."*

Above: Sister Mary Wilson posed with some children in the herb garden at Canterbury, New Hampshire.

BEHOLD THE DAY

The lyrics to "Behold the Day" metaphorically outline the Shaker belief that the Day of Judgment would not occur on a single, undetermined day in the future. Instead, they viewed it "as a work which has already commenced; a work which we ourselves have seen and felt, and tho gradual and progressive in its operations, it is certain and effectual; and will continue to increase in power, till a full and final separation shall be made between good and evil." The Shakers believed that their church represented the second coming of Christ's Church on Earth. Therefore, the time was at hand for each individual to make a choice: join the ranks of the "good," and at the end of the Judgment be harvested to "fill the heavenly garners;" or reject the second coming, and the chance for eternal salvation.

Behold the Day

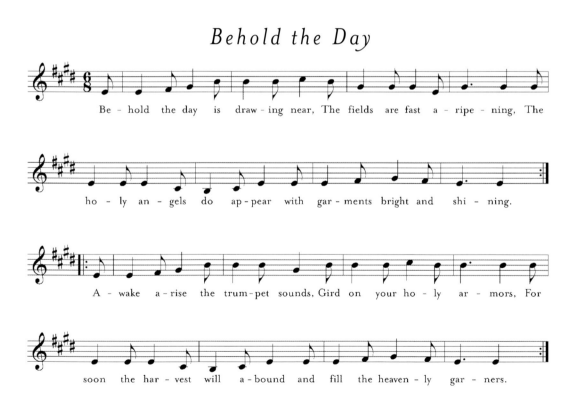

Be - hold the day is draw - ing near, The fields are fast a - ripe - ning, The
ho - ly an - gels do ap - pear with gar - ments bright and shi - ning.
A - wake a - rise the trum - pet sounds, Gird on your ho - ly ar - mors, For
soon the har - vest will a - bound and fill the heaven - ly gar - ners.

O MOTHER
DO RECEIVE ME

"O Mother Do Receive Me" is one of a number of songs given by Native American spirits during the Era of Manifestations. Historically, the Shakers had interacted with Native Americans, especially in the West during the Kentucky Revival. This was especially true at the Busro, Indiana (West Union), community, where the Shawnee

Above: Shaker scribes recorded songs brought by Native spirits in a special, pictograph-like system of Indian musical notation.

Indians were frequent visitors on their way to and from Vincennes before the War of 1812. By the early 1840s native spirits began appearing in Shaker meetings through mediums. They carried with them songs in their "native tongues," as well as native systems for music notation. "O Mother Do Receive Me" is typical of the repertoire, expressing the Indian's desire to reach the eternal reward of Mother's "wigwam in de hebbins abuv."

O Mother Do Receive Me

O de ho - ly shinn-e Mudd - er do ceve me in dy wig -

wam in de hebb - ins. For me will be dood; me will learn to be

dood ob dy chil-dren dat lib on de ground. Me will do any ting dat de white tell me

to, If de Mudd - er will take me wen me do get thro' To lib in her

wig-wam in de hebb-ins a - buv, And wear a crown and a robe of her luv.

INDIAN SONG

The Shakers were interested in the other races that peopled the New World, and many fine songs were received as gifts from Native American and African American spirits. The non-English words were intended to capture the flavor of Indian language. Connoisseurs of early American music may recognize a resemblance between this tune and the nineteenth-century popular song "Shortnin' bread."

Sister Mary Hazard noted on this song, "the two foregoing songs learned of the Chief by John Allen, Sept. 11, 1842."

—The Shakers of Sabbathday Lake

Indian Song

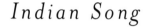

O   me love mo-ther and she loves me.   Quil-le o-se van da   wa-haw me. O

me love mo-ther and   she loves me.   Quil-le o-se van   da   wa - haw me.

Quil-le o-se wah   se   quil-le o-se qua   quil-le o-se qua qua   se me qua.

Qui-le o-se qua   qua   quil-le o-se qua   quil-le o-se qua qua   se me qua.

Above: Sister Mary Hazard (at left) was responsible for recording a substantial portion of the song repertoire at New Lebanon, New York, during the early 1840s.

FOUR LITTLE ANGELS

The early 1840s were a period of intense spiritual activity at the Shaker communities, particularly at the village in New Lebanon, New York. Sister Polly Jane Reed and Sister Mary Hazard have both left us an extraordinary amount of documentary evidence, both visual and musical, of the events of those times.

Above: A Heart-shaped cutout *drawn for Mary Hazard by Polly Jane Reed at New Lebanon, New York, in 1824.*

Polly Jane Reed was born on February 3, 1818, and came to New Lebanon in 1825 at the age of eight. Her parents allowed her to leave home and go with Elder Calvin Green, who was then on a missionary trip in Fairfield, New York. During much of her life she was a tailor, and her hand skills are evidenced by the forty-eight works of art attributed to her. The work at left was one of a series of small hearts, illustrated on both sides in pen and ink, drawn by Sister Polly in the early to mid-1840s. The hearts were tokens of encouragement and reward to her fellow Shakers. Sister Polly was eventually appointed to the Central Ministry in 1868, where she remained until her death on November 25, 1881.

The recipient of the heart at left was Sister Mary Hazard, whose elegantly written songbooks record hundreds of songs received during those years, including "Four Little Angels," and many others contained in this book.

Four Little Angels

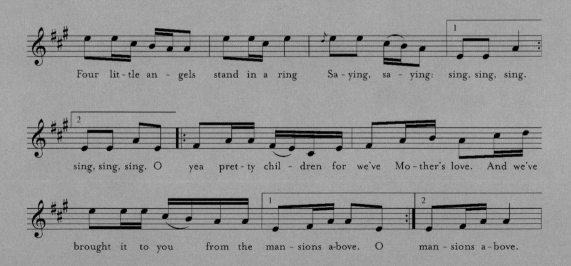

Four lit-tle an - gels stand in a ring Sa - ying, sa - ying: sing, sing, sing.

sing, sing, sing. O yea pret - ty chil - dren for we've Mo - ther's love. And we've

brought it to you from the man - sions a-bove. O man - sions a-bove.

Above: A detail from a Heart-shaped cutout *drawn for Emma Jane Blanchard by Polly Jane Reed at New Lebanon, New York, in 1844.*

CONSOLING DOVE

In the lyrics to this song there are references to two locations—the "Holy Land" and "Chosen Land." Holy Land is the spiritual name of the Alfred, Maine, community, and "Chosen Land" is that of the dwelling at New Gloucester/Sabbathday Lake. This delightful song, preserved in the careful hand of Elder Otis, is a kind of musical greeting card from one village to another. The Sabbathday Lake Shakers believe this piece was sung only once, on the specific occasion of its composition: "Elder Otis received the song [from divine inspiration] and 'gave it out' in the course of the first Meeting in Maine Ministry attended upon their return to Chosen Land." It seems Elder Otis received the tune from a dove—birds are often the bearers of spiritual messages in the Shaker song repertory.

Consoling Dove

THE SAVIOUR'S UNIVERSAL PRAYER

This attractive setting of "The Lord's Prayer" was given at New Lebanon, New York. Although Jesus would seem to have been less venerated by the Shakers than Mother Ann Lee, it is important to remember that both were regarded as earthly vehicles for the same Christ-spirit. The Shakers acknowledged that Jesus was the first coming of Christ, and believed that Mother Ann represented "not the appearance of the same personal Being, but a manifestation of the same Spirit." The key difference between Jesus and Mother Ann lies in the fact that Jesus was the product of a virgin birth, thus leaving him unpolluted by the sin of conception. Jesus was "the first who kept his Father's commandments." Alternately, Mother Ann, having been born of human flesh, bears out the promise that it is possible as a human being to transcend inherent sin and perfect oneself in the image of Christ.

Above: A Tree of Love, a Tree of Life, *drawn by Polly Collins at Hancock, Massachusetts, in 1857.*

The Saviour's Universal Prayer

"Given at the Second Order Feb 15th 1845"

Presto

Our Fa - ther, who art in Heav'n, Hall - ow-ed be thy

name, thy King - dom come, thy will be

done on Earth; as it is done in heaven.

Give us this day our dai - ly bread, and for - give

us our debts, as we for - give our debt - ors.

Leave us not in temp-ta-tion, but de - li-ver us from e - vil, for thine is the

king - dom, the glo - ry and pow - er, for - ev - er more, A - men.

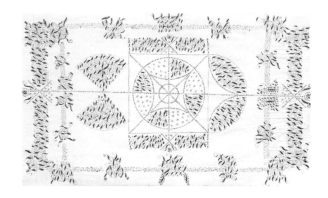

SAMANTHA FAIRBANKS'S ROLL SONG

Samantha (or Semantha) Fairbanks was born on June 16, 1804. She arrived at New Lebanon in 1813 with her widowed mother and five siblings. Sister Samantha grew up in the Church Family and became a Deaconess by 1840. During the Era of Manifestations she periodically entered a state of trance in order to receive and verbalize spirit communications. She is also credited with the execution of six drawings that are categorized as "sacred sheets." Fairbanks eventually rose to the position of Second Eldress in the Central Ministry before her untimely death on March 20, 1852.

Shaker scholar Dr. Daniel Patterson has speculated that some of the sacred sheets were the product of a series of meetings held between January and March of 1843 at New Lebanon. On January 25, "a sheet of clean white paper was handed…to an instrument, or witness for Holy Wisdom's instrument for her angel." Similar sheets were given to the instruments for "the Holy Angel and our Heavenly Parents, likewise the Holy Saviour, who wrote with their fingers, their names upon the white sheet." Patterson believes that these sheets, presumably still blank, were filled in by the instruments over the following weeks. They are some of the most mysterious and fascinating works ever produced by the Shakers.

Samantha Fairbanks's Roll Song

Allegro

O ho - ly ho - ly Fa - ther O ho - ly Heaven-ly Mo -

ther, bless me with thy bless - ing wis - dom

strength and ho - ly pow - er. O ho - ly ho - ly

guar - di - an An - gels, O do my

need - y soul be - friend, and lead my spir - it

on in the prett - y path way my Pa - rents have gone.

Left: Among the earliest of the gift drawings, sacred sheets such as this one—executed by Samantha Fairbanks and Mary Wicks in 1843—are thought to be visual expressions of unknown tongues.

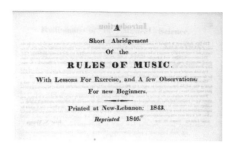

A
Short Abridgement
Of the
RULES OF MUSIC.
With Lessons For Exercise, and A few Observations,
For new Beginners.
Printed at New-Lebanon; 1843.
Reprinted 1846.

ISAAC N YOUNG'S ROLL SONG

Isaac Newton Youngs was born in Johnstown, New York, on July 4th, 1793. He entered the Watervliet, New York, Shaker community in 1803, and eventually moved to New Lebanon, New York, which became his lifelong home. Youngs pursued a variety of interests, including cabinetmaking, tailoring, history, and clockmaking.

Youngs was particularly passionate about music. He worked continuously to develop and refine Shaker music theory, writing in 1830: "It is very desirable to us that Believers should all have one uniform manner of music writing." This desire was fulfilled, as nearly all the communities adopted the system of writing music in small letteral notation, a practice that had been in development since 1816 but that Youngs codified in his 1833 treatise *The Rudiments of Music*. In this system, originally written on a staff, lowercase letters denote pitch, with rhythmic values indicated by hash marks above, below, or through the letter. In 1837 Youngs reported a further refinement to the system: "We have grown into the practice of lessening the labor of writing our new songs by not using the staff, but using common ruled paper." This development could not have come at a more opportune time; with the advent of the Era of Manifestations, new songs, such as "Isaac N Young's Roll Song," were received by the thousands.

Above: The title page from Youngs's first printed treatise A Short Abridgement Of the Rules Of Music, *printed at New Lebanon, New York, in 1843 and 1846.*

Isaac N Young's Roll Song

"Feb. 27th 1845"

Allegro

O my ho-ly hea-ven-ly Fa — ther and Mo —

ther, pro — tect my poor and nee-dy soul I pray

O feed me dail-y with the food I need for

I am whol-ly de-pen-dant. Let me not

wan-der in by and for-bid-den paths, but

lead me on to the man — sions of

peace and im-mor — tal joys.

CHRISTMAS GREETING

The early Shakers were in debate over how to observe Christmas. A wonderful anec-dote in Anna White and Leila S. Taylor's *Shakerism: Its Meaning and Message* explains how the controversy was resolved: "Elder John Hocknell felt an assurance that it should …be observed…not as a day of jesting and frivolity. Hannah Hocknell, on the con-trary, decided…that no particular significance should be attached to it. Accordingly, on the morning of Christmas Day…Hannah arose and began to dress for a day's work at washing and house-cleaning. For some unaccountable reason, she could not get her shoes on….Mother Ann…said this was a sign…" Mother Ann thus decided that the day "be yearly kept and devoted to spiritual purposes." Father Joseph Meacham later stated that the day should be a "grateful remembrance of the open-ing of a door, through the birth of Jesus, for Christ to usher in the era of salvation."

While spiritually in keeping with the first Shakers, early twentieth-century photo-graphs (like the one above) reveal that by the early twentieth century "worldly" decorations had infiltrated some portions of the United Society.

Christmas Greeting

Allegro

Come come learn of me for I am meek and low - ly.

low - ly. O Zi - on a - rise and be rea - dy to meet me, For

lo! I am com-ing with a band of ho - ly An - gels to joy - ful - ly greet

thee.

Come come learn of me for I am meek and low - ly.

Left: Early twentieth-century Christmas decorations at the Brick Dwelling in Hancock, Massachusetts.

COME LET US MARCH

In 1842 a new ritual was instituted first at New Lebanon, New York, and then throughout the rest of the Shaker communities. The ritual came to be known as a "mountain feast." At each village a spot was selected, typically, but not always, on the highest hill adjacent to the community. This spot was cleared of trees and underbrush, leveled, and a small picket enclosure was built. Within this enclosure was placed a marble slab, engraved with "The Word of The Lord." These stones were

Above: An engraving of worship at the Hancock, Massachusetts, "Mount Sinai" feast ground, from Two Years' Experience Among the Shakers *by Shaker apostate Daniel Lamson.*

known as "fountain stones," a name aptly explained by a typical inscription: "THE LORD'S STONE Thus saith Jehovah, Behold! here have I opened a living fountain of holy and eternal waters, for the healing of the nations." The Shakers held elaborate meetings around the fountain stones. During these ceremonies they performed special dances, sang inspired songs, channeled speeches from biblical figures and long-dead Shakers through mediums, ate heavenly fruit, and washed ritualistically in the fountain. These "mountain meetings" gradually fell out of use, and today none of the feast grounds survive intact. "Come Let Us March" seems likely to have been among the repertoire of songs performed on the way to the sacred site. It was recorded by Isaac Newton Youngs, who taught himself the art of engraving in order to inscribe the fountain stone at New Lebanon. Youngs also engraved the Groveland stone, which is the best surviving example of a fountain stone.

Come Let Us March

"May 17th 1846"

Come let us march on our way To the ho-ly moun-tain, There we'll sing, &

there we'll play Round the Chrys-tal foun-tain. There we'll wash & there we'll bathe,

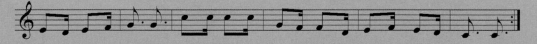

In the liv-ing wa-ters. And in free-dom we'll be-have Like Zi-on's Sons & daught-ers.

SIMPLE GIFTS

"Simple Gifts" is perhaps the most famous of all Shaker songs. Usually attributed to Elder Joseph Brackett of the Maine Ministry, who, with a company of singers, popularized the tune in the summer of 1848.

The concept of spiritual "gifts" is a very important one in Shakerism. "Gifts" can be directions from the spirit to do certain things, sometimes as simple as sweeping, or as dramatic as whirling in place for hours on end. They can also be theological or doctrinal, such as the "gift" to dub each community with a spiritual name and erect a fountain stone on a holy feast ground. Often "gifts" were received as emotional, instructive songs or elaborate drawings. "Gifts" in the Shaker tradition are mutable—they are both given and withdrawn.

Above: A manuscript page showing the song "Simple Gifts" *titled by its form as a Quick Dance.*

Simplicity is a key tenet of Shaker belief. It is reflected in early Shaker architecture, furniture, and dress. Most important, it is manifested in the way that Shakers seek to interact with themselves and others, paring away all that is a hindrance to brotherly/sisterly love. This simplicity is found in meekness before God, and a willingness to bend to divine will and live by the teachings of the Christ spirit, which if followed properly, will bring the soul "round right."

Simple Gifts

'Tis the gift to be sim-ple, 'tis the gift to be free; 'Tis the gift to come down where we ought to be; And when we find our-selves in the place just right, 'Twill be in the val-ley of love and de-light. When true sim-pli-ci-ty is gaind, To bow and to bend we shan't be a-sham'd To turn, turn will be our de-light, 'Till by turn-ing, turn-ing we come round right.

O Come, Come Away

Many Shaker song lyrics contain vocables, which are sequences of sounds without specific meaning upon which a melody can be vocalized. "O Come, Come Away" contains an example of the commonly used Shaker vocable "lo," or "lo-lodle." The majority of Shaker songs that survive from before 1807 are without English texts, but are instead vocalized in unknown tongues or using vocables. This practice dates from the earliest songs sung by Mother Ann Lee, Father William Lee, and Father James Whittaker. Early accounts of Shaker singing describe songs made of "a succession of unmeaning sounds, frequently repeated, half articulated, and plainly gotten by heart." "O Come, Come Away" begins as a texted song, but then reverts to the earlier practice.

O Come, Come Away

Above: The Tree of Light or Blazing Tree, *"seen and received by Hannah Cohoon in the City of Peace [Hancock, Massachusetts] Sabbath Oct 9th 10th hour A.M. 1845."*

MOTHER'S COMFORTING PROMISE

According to the Sabbathday Lake Shakers, this song refers to a specific moment in Shaker history. They explain that it "expressed the deep feelings of tribulation endured by Elder Otis in 1848, when he was asked to leave his position in the Maine Ministry and move to New Gloucester to become their Trustee. This move was necessitated by the apostasy of the former Trustee and lack of any other male capable to take the position in that Society." Even today, conversation at the Shakers' dinner table still occasionally turns to that very difficult moment in the life of the community.

It is interesting to note that "Mother's Comforting Promise" is related musically to the "Holy Order Song"—such melodic borrowings are not unusual in the Shaker repertoire.

Mother's Comforting Promise

I will com-fort them that mourn, Those who weep shall yet re - joice, I will

heal the woun-ded heart, saith your ho-ly Mo-ther's voice.

Above: A detail showing "Mother Ann's Angel of Comfort" from Miranda Barber's 1848 gift drawing
From Holy Mother Wisdom…To Eldress Dana or Mother.

Homily and Kind

Golden Chariot to take
Mother Dana Home.

$48.

WE ARE BORN TO DIE

This rather grim song was recorded by Elder Alonzo Giles Hollister of the Mt. Lebanon Church Family. Brother Alonzo was born on May 24, 1830, and came to the Shakers in 1838 at the age of six. He was variously a chemist, herbalist, bible salesman, and author during the course of his life. "We are Born to Die," which he notated in 1849, is a meditation on the temporary nature of human existence. The singer is reminded that the chief duty while here on earth is to prepare correctly for eternity, "For we are born to die." There are many Shaker songs that ruminate on the topic of death, including a number of funeral hymns written in honor of individual Shakers. Brother Alonzo was only nineteen when he entered "We are Born to Die" into his manuscript hymnal. This is telling not only of the mindset of a young Shaker but also of the constant specter of death that loomed so close in the nineteenth century. Happily, Brother Alonzo lived a long life, and went on to co-author a series of books entitled *Pearly Gate Bible Lessons*, which were question-and-answer books drawing on both traditional Christian and Shaker religious history and theology. Hollister passed away on August 19, 1911, sixty-two years after he notated "We are Born to Die."

We are Born to Die

"Alonzo Hollister, Mt. Lebanon, Chh 1849"

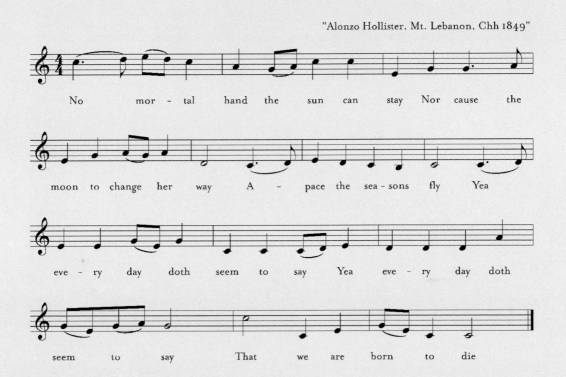

No mor - tal hand the sun can stay Nor cause the

moon to change her way A - pace the sea - sons fly Yea

eve - ry day doth seem to say Yea eve - ry day doth

seem to say That we are born to die

The illustration at left is a detail from Miranda Barber's 1848 drawing From Holy Mother Wisdom…To Eldress Dana or Mother. *It depicts the "Golden Chariot [coming] to take Mother Dana [Eldress Cassandana Goodrich] Home" upon her death, which was sadly imminent at the time of the drawing's execution.*

ALL GLEAN WITH CARE

"All glean with care" is perhaps one of the most powerful Shaker songs. The text is inspired by a number of passages in the *Testimonies of Mother Ann Lee* that concern economy of means. In the *Testimonies* it is noted, "In the time of the harvest, while some of the Brethren were reaping their wheat, Mother Ann sent Elder James into the field to teach them…'Cut your grain clean; God has caused it to grow, and you ought to be careful to save it; for you cannot make one kernel grow, if you know you must starve for the want of it.'"

Elder Otis [Sawyer] noted at the end of this song, "The foregoing hymn was written in gold and purple letters and placed upon the gate posts leading into the Feast Ground upon the holy Mount. The same was engraved upon a gold and silver trumpet which was taken from off the Altar of truth on the Holy Mountain at New Lebanon, June 12, 1850." What Elder Otis is describing is a vision seen and recorded by an inspired Shaker (Instrument). The hymn and description was sent in a letter to the Maine Ministry from the Lebanon Ministry.

—The Shakers at Sabbathday Lake

All glean with care

1. Glean your or-chards, glean your gar-dens, Glean o glean in God-ly fear,
2. Yet my judge-ments those most aw-ful I with-hold by my right hand,
3. Do go forth in might and pow-er Gat-her fruit and herb-age all,
4. Look ye well to fence your pas-tures And your moor-ing fields in - close;

With a pru-dent care-ful spi-rit Save some for the co-ming years.
That my peo-ple may take war-ning Though I send forth no com-mand.
Which I give for life's sub-sis-tence: Save of such both great and small.
See that nought in your pos-ses-sions Lie ex-posed to waste what grows.

For my hand saith the Al-migh-ty, I shall wave from pole to pole;
Still my hand saith the Al-migh-ty, I shall wave from pole to pole;
For my hand, saith the Al-migh-ty, I shall wave from pole to pole;
For my hand, saith the Al-migh-ty I shall wave from pole to pole;

Know ye that the time is co-ming, You have need to save the whole.
O pray Zi-on do take war-ning, Be ye pru-dent, save the whole.
Know the time is rol-ling on-ward When you'll need to save the whole.
Wait no long-er Zi-on's chil-dren, Now's the time to save the whole.

(two more strophes; a few rhythms altered)

Left: Elder Otis Sawyer (1815–1884) of the Maine ministry traveled between the Alfred and Sabbathday Lake Shaker communities throughout his life.

Holy Faith

The Era of Manifestations resulted in the reception of many "gifts" by the Shakers. Among these were the songs known as anthems—spontaneous, rhapsodic songs that were often transmitted through a community member from a denizen of the spirit world. Similar in nature to gift drawings or inspired writings, these songs had wandering melodies and exalted language. The proliferation—and importance—of such songs prompted Elder Henry C. Blinn of Canterbury, New Hampshire, to set many in printed letteral notation for his 1852 book, *A Sacred Repository of Anthems and Hymns.*

"Holy Faith" was received at Union Village, Ohio, probably sometime in the mid 1840s. In a later publication Blinn described the way in which such songs were "given": "Young men and women became the willing or unwilling subjects of this new and strange visitation. During their journeys to the more spiritual sphere, they became the active mediums for singing the most beautiful pieces of music, and in their exaltation, their descriptive language was remarkably increased, as they related their wonderful visits to the spirit land, and pictured the lovely mansions prepared for the faithful in Christ."

Right: The title page from A Sacred Repository of Anthems and Hymns, *the first full-length Shaker music imprint set in letteral notation.*

A

SACRED REPOSITORY

OF

ANTHEMS AND HYMNS,

FOR

DEVOTIONAL WORSHIP AND PRAISE.

I will praise the name of God with a song, and will magnify him with thanksgiving.   *Psalms*, lxix. 30.

Canterbury, N. H.
1852.

Holy Faith

Allegro

O — — — bless - ed gos - pel thou art e - ter - nal;

thou — wilt en - dure when time shall — be no — more; thou

wilt en - dure when — t - i - m - e — shall — be no more.

O my soul! O my soul, keep thy faith most ho - - -

ly, for - ev - er and ev - er. What though grief and sor - row fill thy

way, and an - gry bill - ows on thee — r - o - l - l; yet

God is just and truth shall stand to bear thee safe - ly — home.

Be — ye of good cheer, be — ye of good — cheer dear Breth - ren and

Sis - ters, — for though the wi - cked flou - rish as a green

tree, yet I know saith the Lord, it shall be well -

with the right - eous. Then ne - ver look to

So - dom's dis - mal plains, to find a hi - ding place, but keep your

course on Zi - on - ward, and God will be your guide.

Heart rend - ing thoughts! Aw - ful! aw - ful! aw - ful!!!

for - those who sell their ho - ly birth - right, and sink their souls for -

ev - er! Draw near, O Lord, we crave thy strength,

we need thy sa - ving power, O grant it Lord, we

hum - bly pray; O let thy hea-ven-ly gifts flow down, Like a foun-tain of

wa - ters; Grant the pure in heart a crown, Zi - on's Sons and Daught - ers.

JOYFUL PRAISES

This beautiful, dance-like hymn came from the community in South Union, Kentucky, but also appears in the New Hampshire-produced *A Sacred Repository of Anthems and Hymns*. As is generally the case in Shaker music, the biblically inspired metaphors refer to the Shakers themselves and their specific beliefs. The basic theme, as the Sabbathday Lake Shakers point out, is the fulfillment of the Promised Land. The flames of the furnace, evoked in the last strophe, do not destroy gold, and so the Shakers believed they would survive all earthly tribulation.

Joyful Praises

1. Sing, ye Mother's sons and daughters Who in love together dwell,
2. See the milk and honey flowing Taste the clusters of the vine;
3. Fear not, says the God of Zion Neither let thy hand be slack;
4. Though the fields should all be dried, Trying scenes afflict the fold,

And who drink the living waters Out of the celestial well;
Precious love and union growing, Here we have the choicest wine.
Though the scenes are often trying Strength the city shall not lack.
All that's in the furnace tried Never can affect the gold.

Praise the God of our salvation who hath made out feet to stand,
We shall no more be ashamed, Pride has to be overthrown;
For the Lord the God is Holy Mighty in the midst of thee;
God has brought the restoration, We are fixed in the rock;

In the midst of desolation O the blessed promised land.
Here are called the poor and maimed All the humble God will own.
In his love shall rest the lowly, in his spirit they'll be free.
Strength and glory of the nation Praises sing ye little flock.

Left: Elder Henry C. Blinn of the Canterbury, New Hampshire Shakers, shown here tending his bees.

Above: A Bower of Mulberry Trees, *"seen and painted in the City of Peace [Hancock, Massachusetts] by Hannah Cohoon"* in 1854.

THANKSGIVING

The Shakers used many "worldly" tunes as the basis for new lyrics of their own cre-ation. For instance, the pentatonic melody of "Thanksgiving" is related to that of the English ballad "Barbara Allen." Early Shaker dance tunes were often undisguised, vocalized versions of fiddle tunes then popular throughout the Western world. In fact, the earliest written account of English Shaker worship published in America, which appeared in the *Virginia Gazette* in 1769 (prior to the sect's emigration to America), sarcastically recounts that the Shakers would sing and dance "to the pious tunes of Nancy Dawson, Bobbin Joan, Hie thee Jemmy home again, &c." As Shaker scholar Dr. Daniel Patterson has pointed out, many other Shaker tunes have their origins in the traditional balladry of the British Isles.

Thanksgiving

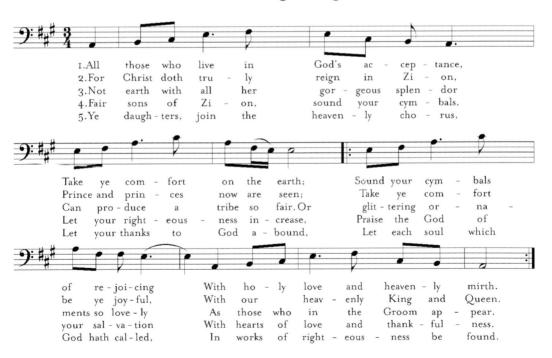

VOICE OF THE ANGEL OF MERCY

This vigorous, prophetic hymn is the last one in *A Sacred Repository of Anthems and Hymns*, the tome that was typeset in letteral notation and printed at the Canterbury, New Hampshire, village in 1842. The songs in the *Repository* are often longer and more difficult than those found in other mid-nineteenth century manuscripts. These pieces were evidently held in special esteem, but were perhaps deemed harder to learn and perform from memory alone. The annotation to "Voice of the Angel of Mercy" reads, "Given by inspiration, 1850."

Right: The letteral notation used in the 1852 songbook A Sacred Repository of Anthems and Hymns.

VOICE OF THE ANGEL OF MERCY.

Fear not fear not, my be-loved few, Though the trump
of war may sound, And destruction may roll from the center
to the pole, And devastation lie all a-round; For surely I,
for surely I, Who have brought you from Egyptian darkness,

Voice of the Angel of Mercy

Fear not fear not my be - lo - ved few, Though the trump of war may sound, And de - struc - tion may roll from the cen - ter to the pole, And de - va - sta - tion lie all a - round; For sure - ly I, for sure - ly I, who have brought you from E - gyp - tian dark - ness Will your - souls pro - tect while you do res - pect And fol - low my laws with ex - act - ness. For act - ness. I'll cause the moun - tains of earth to de - scend And the hum - ble val - leys to a - rise, And the fab - rics of man as the dust I will fan, for his sys - tems I do des - pise. And sure - ly I, and sure - ly I, who es -

tab - lish - ed the earth's foun - da - tion, Will spread o'er her face the

know - ledge of grace, And the king - dom of full sal - va - tion For va - tion

Then in mer - cy be warned O my peo - ple to walk In the

strict - ness of my ho - ly spi - rit And thus ye shall stand, when af -

flic - tions fill the land, And my ho - ly bless - ings in - he - rit. Yea

sure - ly know, yea sure - ly know, Though thou - sands ar - rive to op -

pose you, I will con - quer the foe, turn in - ward the blow, And my

house shall re - main un - sca - thed. Yea sca - thed.

THE BLESSINGS
OF PEACE

"The Blessings of Peace" is a fine and moving example of a Shaker anthem. Like its antecedents in music history—the New England anthem, the baroque motet, and the Renaissance madrigal—the Shaker anthem is a through-composed genre, setting each line of text to new music. Less well known than the Shaker hymns and spirituals, the anthems nonetheless contain some of the finest poetical and musical inspirations of these religious communities. The words of the following anthem were taken from the influential Shaker treatise *The Testimony of Christ's Second Appearing*, which was published in 1808; the tune was composed at New Lebanon, New York.

Right: A detail from An Emblem of the Heavenly Sphere *showing "a fountain of living water."*

The Blessings of Peace

What mil-lions from se-ques-tered val-leys and de-so-late moun-tains, from lone-ly cot-ta-ges and si-lent groves, From tor-ture-rooms and racks and de-vou-ring flames, have look-ed and wept, and pray-ed toward this lat-ter day of li-ber-ty and peace. How have they talked of the rights of man, and la-bored to de-scribe in words what our eyes be-hold, and our souls [do] dai-ly [dai-ly] en-joy; name-ly; the bles-sings the bles-sings the bles-sings of peace and sal-va-tion in a land sa-cred to free-dom. Then how un-speak-ab-ly great is our priv-e-lege! See-ing the eyes of of all see-ing the eyes of all who have

HOLY HABITATION

Composed in New Lebanon, New York, "Holy Habitation" is a hymn of thanksgiving that is rich in Biblical imagery. The text, as the extant Shakers now remark, points to "the rewards to those who would maintain a Shaker life." The nature metaphors of this and other Shaker songs take on an even greater resonance when one realizes that, even today, the Shaker community continues to carefully cultivate a balance with and respect for the environment.

Above: A celestial Shaker dwelling from Polly Jane Reed's 1849 work
A present from Mother Lucy to Eliza Ann Taylor.

Holy Habitation

(quick and vigorous)

1. Lord, thy name shall be ex - al - ted By the hum - ble and the pure;
2. Fill my soul with true thanks-giv - ing, Fill my mouth with songs of praise;
3. Bles - sed way of free sal - va - tion! Bles - sed cross that we main - tain!
4. Can I e - ver fret or mur-mur, Or be life - less dull or cold,
5. Here the ten - der vine and myr - tle Spread sweet o - dors all a - round,

Thou hast ga - thered her that hal - ted, Thou art cal - ling in the poor;
Those who feel their spi - rits liv - ing Ev - ery grate - ful feel - ing raise.
Prize the ho - ly ha - bi - ta - tion, Where these gifts of God re - main.
Where an e - ver las - ting sum - mer Such fine beau - ties does un - fold?
Love - ly vir - gins dance in cir - cles To the harp's me - lod-ious sound.

Thou dost com - fort the af - flic - ted, And re - lieve the fa - ther - less,
Rise my soul re - joice for - ev - er, Prize the res - ur - rec - tion morn;
Bles - sed food how sweet and plea-sant! Bles - sed is our heaven - ly fare;
Here's the oil and wine in - vi - ting, Here the milk and ho - ney flow;
Ho - ly an - gels guard my spi - rit In the path the Sa - vior trod,

Help - less or - phans are pro - tec - ted in the way of ho - li - ness.
Praise the hand that formed my Mo-ther, praise the day that she was born.
When the love of God is pre-sent It is hea - ven ev - ery - where.
Ma - ny pre - cious gifts u - ni - ting, Here the bloo-ming li - lies grow.
That I might a right in - her - it On the ho - ly mount of God.

ROUND IN 3 PARTS

The Shakers spent a considerable amount of time developing their music theory. The leaders in this field were Russell Haskell of Enfield, Connecticut, and Isaac Newton Youngs of New Lebanon, New York. Youngs published his *Short Abridgment of the Rules of Music* in 1843, while Haskell's *A Musical Expositor* was published in 1847. Both men embraced the letteral notation system, but they argued endlessly on the tonic pitch for the minor mode. Haskell believed that minor tunes should begin on "D," while Youngs (and practically everyone else) maintained that "A" was the root of the natural minor mode. Setting the finer points of music theory aside, Shaker treatises on music contain some interesting experiments, such as the accompanying round. The date of this song's manuscript is unknown, but it is likely from before 1860. The Shakers rarely used harmony before the 1870s, making this round a rather unique example. When this tune is performed, the first singer starts at the beginning, the second begins when the first has reached a spot indicated in the music as "2nd," and the third, when the first has reached the spot marked "3rd."

Right: This manuscript of unknown date and authorship contains numerous musical exercises, both theoretical and practical.

Round In 3 Parts

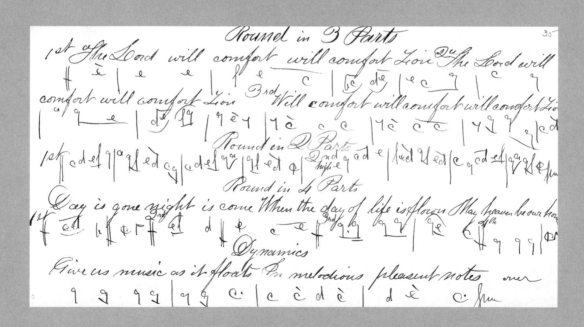

O ZION ARISE

The westernmost Shaker community at South Union, Kentucky, was populated mostly by converts won during the Kentucky Revival (ca.1805), many of whom were slaveholders. Typically, new members would dissolve the master-slave relationship, which placed them in an unfamiliar relationship of brotherhood. This was not an easy transition, and the racial stereotypes of the day were certainly not absent from South Union. These attitudes were reflected in the creation of a separate "Black Family" at South Union, with a former slave named Neptune in the Elder's position. While Shakers freely accepted African Americans into their membership, there was some difficulty reconciling slavery with Shakerism. This internal conflict is evident in *South Union Journal A*: "April 1816, Sat. 27 BRO'T Back—Sam'l Stelle went & bro't Back from Tom Proctor's the obstinate yellow boy Mose— ...taken out there to learn a little of slavery, or to get his haughty spirit reduced" and later, "Sept. 24, 1829 Negroes being driven south today—two and two chained together with a short chain to keep them from skedaddling. Does God see this? Rather think he does."

Years after these journal entries were made Sister Betsy Smith of South Union penned "O Zion Arise," a song that boldly pronounces the Shaker gospel's embrace of "All kindreds, all colors, all nations and people."

Above: A photograph taken circa 1900 of Shakers in front of the 1847 East House at South Union, Kentucky.

O Zion Arise

O Zi - on a - rise like a beau - ti - ful mor - ning, And
Here Li - ber - ty reigns as the stan - dard of un - ion And

let thy fair bright - ness at - tend thee a - broad. For all shall con -
all are in - vi - ted to ga - ther a - round And share in the

fess it in earth and in hea - ven That thou has de - scen - ded from
bles - sings pre - par - ed by hea - ven For no o - ther good like to

no - one but God. Though ma - ny in rage may re - mon - strate a
it can be found. All kin - dreds, all co - lors, all na - tions all

gainst thee, Thy ho - ly foun - da - tion for - ev - er shall
peo - ple, No na - tion or sect are re - jec - ted at

stand, Un - sul - lied by slan - der, re - proach or by en - vy U -
all. But all who are wil - ling to give up their i - dols U -

pon this fair soil of A - mer - i - ca's land.
pon this fair Zi - on of God they may call.

A FAITHFUL CHILD

The inscription that follows "A Faithful Child" in the manuscript is particularly interesting: "The manner in which the above song was given was peculiar. It was learned from a little bright light that moved around [Deacon Stephen Munson's] head a few inches off." The song is recorded in one of Mary Hazard's hymnals, which are among the best collections of gift songs received during the Era of Manifestations. Hazard was diligent about noting not just the melodies and lyrics, but also the circumstances surrounding the songs' reception. Songs were received in a variety of different—and perhaps to modern sensibilities, strange—ways during the late 1830s and throughout the 1840s. Sister Mary's note that a "bright light" bringing a song was "peculiar" provides some measure of insight—for an otherworldly manifestation to be considered unusual during that spiritually active time suggests that the manner of this song's reception must have been strange indeed.

Above: Mother Ann's Word to her little child, Elizabeth Cantrell, *drawn at New Lebanon, New York, by Miranda Barber in 1848.*

A Faithful Child

"From Mother Ann, to Deacon
Stephen Munson. July 25th 1839."

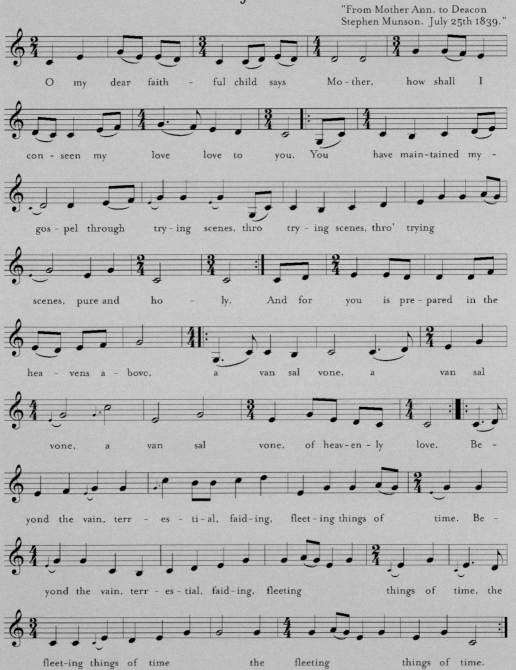

O my dear faith - ful child says Mo - ther, how shall I

con - seen my love love to you. You have main-tained my -

gos - pel through try - ing scenes, thro try - ing scenes, thro' trying

scenes, pure and ho - ly. And for you is pre - pared in the

hea - vens a - bove, a van sal vone, a van sal

vone, a van sal vone, of heav-en - ly love. Be -

yond the vain, terr - es - ti - al, faid-ing, fleet-ing things of time. Be -

yond the vain, terr - es - tial, faid-ing, fleeting things of time, the

fleet-ing things of time the fleeting things of time.

FAREWELL
DEAR CROSSBEARERS

The Shakers were great travelers—some traveled for business, some to share skills and technology with other communities, and in later years, some traveled for pleasure. Among the greatest Shaker travelers were the members of the Ministry, who were the spiritual leaders of different Bishoprics. (An example would be the Hancock Bishopric, which was comprised of the communities of Hancock and Tyringham,

Above: The Round Stone Barn at Hancock, Massachusetts—one of the most unique buildings at the Shaker village— was revolutionary in its efficient, circular design.

Massachusetts, and Enfield, Connecticut.) Ultimately, each Bishopric was overseen spiritually by the Central Ministry at Mt. Lebanon, New York. However, on a local level, each Bishopric had its own Ministry, composed of two Elders and two Eldresses. The members of the Ministry were the highest authority on all matters and often traveled to the communities under their care multiple times a year. A large body of songs dedicated to them survives—these were composed either upon the Ministry's arrival at, or departure from, various Shaker villages. "Farewell Dear Crossbearers" was recorded by a scribe at Hancock around 1850 and is also known as the "Hancock Farewell." The tune is derived from a "worldly" folk song known as "The Wagoner's Lad."

Farewell Dear Crossbearers

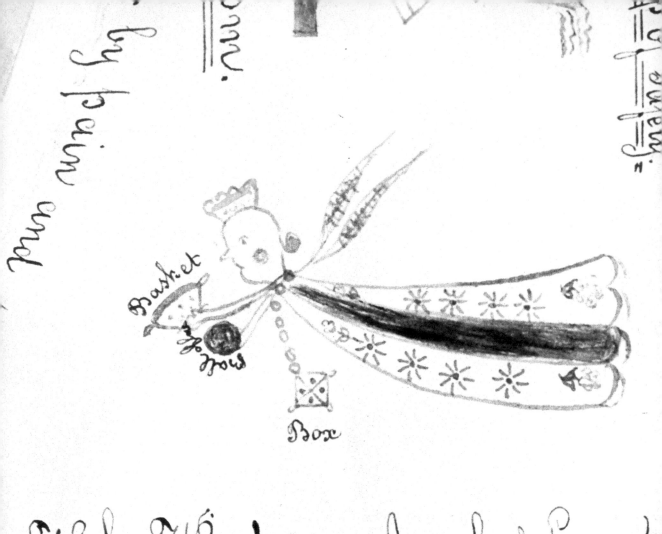

Above: "Holy Wisdom's Angel of Love" from Miranda Barber's 1848 work, From Holy Mother Wisdom...
To Eldress Dana or Mother.

SWEET ANGELS COME NEARER

The older Shaker Sisters at Sabbathday Lake remember this song from communal singing earlier in the century; it was also printed, in four harmonized parts, in a later hymnal from Canterbury, New Hampshire. The melody was apparently adapted from an earlier song by Elder Otis Sawyer that was discovered in the Sabbathday Lake archive in June of 2000. The Shakers now believe that the melody originated in the Alfred, Maine, community.

Sweet angels come nearer

Sweet An - gels come near - er O near - er and near - er Do list to our plead - ing for strength from on high. This world's seem - ing pleas - sures, Its rich - es and ho - nors The im - mor - tal Spi - rit can ne - ver sup - ply.

THE ANGEL REAPERS

This beautiful spiritual is a post-Civil War piece, differing in some respects from earlier Shaker songs. There is a revival-song influence to be heard here, perhaps in keeping with its Southern provenance (the Sabbathday Lake Shakers believe a South Union, Kentucky, scribe learned this song on an 1869 trip to the eastern communities). The song's promise that loved ones will be reunited in "the land of the Golden Harvest" is important to Shaker belief, and the marvelous upward sweep of the melody from low to high is characteristic of Shaker music.

The Angel Reapers

The an-gels of light are rea-ping the world, With a sick-le of love they will ga-ther In-

to the trea-su-ry of the hea-ven a-bove The ran-somed souls of the har-vest.

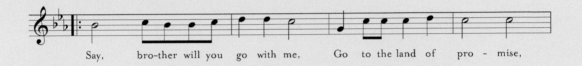

Say, bro-ther will you go with me, Go to the land of pro-mise,

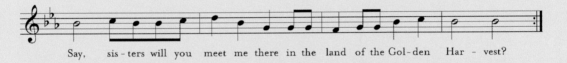

Say, sis-ters will you meet me there in the land of the Gol-den Har-vest?

(some pitches altered)

Left: A Heart-shaped cutout drawn for Amy Reed by Polly Jane Reed at New Lebanon, New York, in 1844.

PATH OF SORROW

"Path of Sorrow" is a fitting choice to end this collection of Shaker songs. The lyrics honor the sacrifices made by those individuals who lived their lives in the Christ spirit by the example of both Jesus and Mother Ann (referred to, respectively, as the "Lamb and Bride"). From their earliest days facing persecution in New England, through their great expansion into the West and ultimate rise to social prominence and progressive leadership, the Shaker movement has maintained its core principles. As Brother Arnold Hadd of the Sabbathday Lake Shakers explains, the focus of a Shaker life is "to take up a cross against all those things that God cannot own nor bless, such as selfishness, jealousy, anger, hatred, [and] prejudice." Choosing to live as a Shaker cannot be an easy choice, but our religious and cultural heritage has been greatly enriched by the legacy of those who have made that choice. That the Shakers of Sabbathday Lake reintroduced the hymn "Path of Sorrow" in the year 2000, more than 150 years after its composition, is a testament to the ongoing growth and continuity of the Shaker tradition.

Above: A view of the Church Family dwelling at the Alfred, Maine, Shaker community by Brother Joshua Bussell in the 1870s.

Path Of Sorrow

1.Rise my soul for in-spi-ra-tion, Wakes the sol-emn call for thee;
2.Think ye not the way is rough-er Then when Je-sus went be-fore,
3.Tru-ly bles-sings then were gi-ven An-gels in their hearts sus-tain,
4.[Though] Thy path is paved with sor-row Oft be-dew'd with ma-ny tears,

O pre-pare for tri-bu-la-tion this thy cer-tain lot shall be.
Think what mo-ther had to suf-fer What her faith-ful fol-low-ers bore.
While the dread-ful wrath of hea-ven It de-scen-ded like the rain.
Bear thee on to-day to-mor-row God may ban-ish all thy fears.

God has pro-mised no ex-emp-tion But his chil-dren must be tried,
On the cross be-hold him lan-guish, While a scoff-ing world sur-rounds;
When tho' grief thy soul de-press-es Rol-ling o'er thee like the waves,
Hope in him for thou shalt praise him So shalt ev'-ry ho-nest soul,

All who share the great re-demp-tion Pur-chased by the Lamb and Bride.
Think of Mo-ther's bit-ter an-guish In her i-cy pri-son bound.
Still re-mem-ber him that bles-ses, Still re-gard the hand that saves.
He who loves, be-lieves o-beys him While un-cea-sing a-ges roll.

Song Sources

The songs that appear in this book were transcribed by Christian Goodwillie and Joel Cohen from original manuscripts, which are held in a variety of collections (please see the Abbreviation Key below for collection names).

Abbreviation Key:

DWt: Delaware, Winterthur Library
KBGK : Kentucky, Bowling Green,
    The Kentucky Library
MPBA: Massachusetts, Pittsfield,
    The Berkshire Athenaeum
MPH: Massachusetts, Pittsfield,
    Hancock Shaker Village, Inc.
OCWR: Ohio, Cleveland, The Western Reserve
    Historical Society
MeSL: Maine, Sabbathday Lake,
    The United Society of Shakers
WLCM: Washington, D.C.,
    The Library of Congress

Mother Ann's Song: *MeSL, 10-MU-040, p. 171; transcribed by Joel Cohen*
Trumpet of Peace: *A Sacred Repository of Anthems and Hymns, Canterbury, NH, 1852, p. 105; transcribed by Joel Cohen*
Solemn Song of the Ancients: *MeSL, 14-MU-060, p. (15); transcribed by Joel Cohen*
Stone Prison: *MeSL, 10-MU-040, #71, p. 54; transcribed by Joel Cohen*
Rights of Conscience: *WLCM, M/2131/.S4E5 p. 221; transcribed by Joel Cohen*
Holy Order Song: *MeSL, 14-MU-040, #466; transcribed by Joel Cohen*
The Testimony of Eternal Truth: *WLCM, M/2131/.S4E5 p. 227; transcribed byChristian Goodwillie*
The Tree of Life: *WLCM, M/2131/.S4E5 p. 218; transcribed by Christian Goodwillie*
Revival Song: *KBGK, South Union Shaker Journal A, p. 216; transcribed by Christian Goodwillie*
The Midnight Cry: *OCWR, SM 255 p. 10; transcribed by Christian Goodwillie*
Untitled Dance Tune: *MeSL, 25-MU-10;*

transcribed by Joel Cohen
Spiritual Wine: *WLCM, M/2131/.S4E5 p. 225; transcribed by Christian Goodwillie*
Industry: *MPH, 9775 #1081 p. 61b,c; transcribed by Christian Goodwillie*
The Harvest: *MeSL, LCM-M/2131; transcribed by Joel Cohen*
A Quick Song: *MPH, 9775 # 882 p. 13r, v; transcribed by Christian Goodwillie*
A HYMN COMPOSED...: *OCWR, SM 246; transcribed by Christian Goodwillie*
Song of Colovin: *DWt, Edward Deming Andrews Memorial Shaker Collection #896 p. 123; transcribed by Christian Goodwillie*
Call for Love: *OCWR, SM 247 p. 13; transcribed by Christian Goodwillie*
Blessing and Love: *OCWR, SM 247 p. 46; transcribed by Christian Goodwillie*
Christopher Columbus's March: *OCWR, SM 247; transcribed by Christian Goodwillie*
Angel of Love: *OCWR, SM 247; transcribed by Christian Goodwillie*
Behold the Day: *MeSL, 10-MU-040, #225*
O Mother do receive me: *DWt, Edward Deming Andrews Memorial Shaker Collection #847 p. 87; transcribed by Christian Goodwillie*
Indian Song: *MeSL, 10-MU-040, #129; transcribed by Joel Cohen*
I Am an Angel of Light: *MeSL, 17-MU-050; transcribed by Joel Cohen*
Four Little Angels: *MeSL, 10-MU-040; transcribed by Joel Cohen*
Consoling Dove: *MeSL, 14-MU-047, p. 10; transcribed by Joel Cohen*
The Savior's Universal Prayer: *MPBA, Vol. 12; transcribed by Christian Goodwillie*
Samantha Fairbanks's Roll Song: *MPBA, Vol. 12 p. 12-13; transcribed by Christian Goodwillie*
Isaac N. Young's Roll Song: *MPBA, Vol. 12 p. 18; transcribed by Christian Goodwillie*
Christmas Greeting: *MPBA, Vol. 12 p. 57; transcribed by Christian Goodwillie*
Come Let Us March: *MPH, 9775 Y725 #1082, Song #114; transcribed by Christian Goodwillie*

I Am a Bright Lark: *MPH, 9775 Y725 #1082, Song #135; transcribed by Christian Goodwillie*
Simple Gifts: *MPBA, Vol. 18; transcribed by Christian Goodwillie*
Mother's Comforting Promise: *MeSL, 14-MU-047; transcribed by Joel Cohen*
We Are Born to Die: *MPH #9775, #1081*
All Glean with Care: *MeSL, 1-MU-025, #31; transcribed by Joel Cohen*
Holy Faith: *A Sacred Repository of Anthems and Hymns, Canterbury, NH, 1852, p. 18; transcribed by Christian Goodwillie*
Joyful Praises: *A Sacred Repository of Anthems and Hymns, Canterbury, NH, 1852, p. 72; transcribed by Joel Cohen*
Thanksgiving: *A Sacred Repository of Anthems and Hymns, Canterbury, NY 1852, p. 148; transcribed by Joel Cohen*
Voice of the Angels of Mercy: *A Sacred Repository of Anthems and Hymns, Canterbury, NY 1852, p. 221; transcribed by Joel Cohen*
The Blessings of Peace: *A Sacred Repository of Anthems and Hymns, Canterbury, NY 1852, p. 9; transcribed by Joel Cohen*
Holy Habitation: *A Sacred Repository of Anthems and Hymns, Canterbury, NY 1852, p. 18; transcribed by Joel Cohen*
Round in 3 Parts: *MPH, 9775.A1 #318 p. 35; transcribed by Christian Goodwillie*
Negro Songs: *MeSL, 14-MU-035, #15. 10-MU-040, #168; transcribed by Joel Cohen*
O Zion Arise: *MeSL, 17-MU-020, p. 5; transcribed by Joel Cohen*
A Faithful Child: *DWt, Edward Deming Andrews Memorial Shaker Collection #896; transcribed by Christian Goodwillie*
Farewell Dear Crossbearers: *MPH #9775, #900; transcribed by Deborah Rentz-Moore*
Sweet Angels Come Nearer: *MeSL, 17-MU-110, p. 29 (entitled "A Prayer"); transcribed by Joel Cohen*
The Angel Reapers: *MeSL, 17-MU-110, p. 38; transcribed by Joel Cohen*
The Path of Sorrow: *MeSL, 1-MU-025, #17; transcribed by Joel Cohen*

Art Sources

Polly Collins, *An Emblem of the Heavenly Sphere*, 1854, courtesy of Hancock Shaker Village

Isaac Hutton (1766-1855): *Plan of the City of Albany Surveyed by Simeon DeWitt (Detail of the Courthouse and Prison)*; engraving on paper, 1794; Albany Institute of History & Art Library; Bequest of Ledyard Cogswell, Jr.

Millennial Praises, 1812-1813, courtesy of Hancock Shaker Village

Millennial Laws, 1821, courtesy of Hancock Shaker Village

The Whirling Gift, 1848, courtesy of Hancock Shaker Village

Richard McNemar, *Title page from The Kentucky Revival*, 1808, courtesy of Hancock Shaker Village

Hannah Cohoon, *The Tree of Life*, 1854, courtesy of Hancock Shaker Village

The Midnight Cry, 1870, courtesy of Hancock Shaker Village

Blue Shoe, courtesy of Hancock Shaker Village

Wine Labels, courtesy of Hancock Shaker Village

Stereoview of Sisters from Enfield, Connecticut, courtesy of Hancock Shaker Village

Stereoview of Brother Levi Shaw, courtesy of Hancock Shaker Village

Shakers, Their Mode of Worship, circa 1830, courtesy of Hancock Shaker Village

Ann Lee's gravestone, courtesy of Christian Goodwillie

Unknown, *Dove with rings*, courtesy of Hancock Shaker Village

A Singing Meeting, 1885, courtesy of Hancock Shaker Village

Sarah Bates, *From Holy Mother Wisdom to Sarah Ann Standish*, 1847, courtesy of Hancock Shaker Village

Polly Collins, *Wreath brought by Mother's little dove*, 1853, courtesy of Hancock Shaker Village

Polly Jane Reed, *A present from Mother Lucy to Eliza Ann Taylor*, 1849, courtesy of Hancock Shaker Village

Stereoview of Sister Mary Wilson in the garden at Canterbury, New Hampshire, courtesy of Hancock Shaker Village

Indian notation, courtesy of Winterthur Estate

Photograph of Sister Mary Hazard, courtesy of Hancock Shaker Village

Stereoview of the Second Meeting House at New Lebanon, New York, courtesy of Hancock Shaker Village

Polly Jane Reed, *Heart-shaped cutout...to Mary Hazard*, 1844, courtesy of Hancock Shaker Village

Polly Jane Reed, *Heart-shaped cutout...to Emma Jane*, 1844, courtesy of Hancock Shaker Village

Polly Collins, *A Tree of Love, A Tree of Life*, 1857, courtesy of Hancock Shaker Village

Samantha Fairbanks and Mary Wicks, *Sacred Sheet*, 1843, courtesy of Hancock Shaker Village

A Short Abridgement Of the Rules of Music, courtesy of Hancock Shaker Village

Christmas decorations at the Brick Dwelling at Hancock, Massachusetts, courtesy of Hancock Shaker Village

Mountain Meeting, courtesy of Hancock Shaker Village

Miranda Barber, *From Holy Mother Wisdom...To Eldress Dana or Mother*, 1848, courtesy of Hancock Shaker Village

Manuscript page of "Quick Dance," courtesy of The Berkshire Athenaeum

Hannah Cohoon, *The Tree of Light or Blazing Tree*, 1845, courtesy of Hancock Shaker Village

Photograph of Elder Otis Sawyer, courtesy of Hancock Shaker Village

Pages from *A Sacred Repository of Anthems and Hymns*, courtesy of Hancock Shaker Village

Photograph of Elder Henry C. Blinn, courtesy of Hancock Shaker Village

Hannah Cohoon, *A Bower of Mulberry Trees*, 1854, courtesy of Hancock Shaker Village

Manuscript page of "Round in 3 Parts," courtesy of Hancock Shaker Village

Photograph of Sister Phoebe Lane, courtesy of The Western Reserve Historical Society

Historic Photograph of 1847 East House with Group of Five Shakers, including John Perryman, 1900, courtesy of Shaker Museum at South Union, Kentucky

Miranda Barber, *Mother Ann's Word to her little child*, Elizabeth Cantrell, 1848, courtesy of Hancock Shaker Village

Stereoview of the Round Stone Barn at Hancock, Massachusetts, courtesy of Hancock Shaker Village

Polly Jane Reed, *A Heart-shaped cutout...to Amy Reed*, 1844, courtesy of Hancock Shaker Village

Joshua Bussell, *View of the Church Family*, 1870s, courtesy of Hancock Shaker Village

Additional photography by Michael Fredericks

Acknowledgments

I would like to thank Mom, Dad, and Quinn, for all the love and support and encouragement to pursue my interests, Matt Janeski for technical assistance, Dr. Magda Gabor-Hotchkiss for dedicated research assistance, Dr. Daniel Patterson for reviewing the introduction and answering questions along the way, Dr. Jane Crosthwaite for reviewing the manuscript, Brother Arnold Hadd for clarifying the finer points of Shaker theology, Lawrence J. Yerdon for an incredible opportunity, David Newell for the tip on "The Midnight Cry," Deborah Rentz-Moore for permission to use her transcription of "Farewell Dear Crossbearers," Tommy Hines, Kathleen Reilly, and Jeanne Solensky for their cheerful help in getting illustrations, Deborah Burns for her insightful advice, and Mary Ann Haagen for her encouragement of my interest in Shaker music. Last but not least, I'd like to thank Joel Cohen for bringing these songs to life, Steve Leroy for his careful attention to detail in setting the songs, J.P. Leventhal for his creative energy, and Kylie Foxx, for her patience, editorial skill, and accusing me of hubris.

Performance Acknowledgments

The accompanying compact disk features performances by The Boston Camerata, Joel Cohen, director; members of the Harvard University Choir, Murray Somerville, director; members of Youth Pro Musica, Hazel Somerville, director; and The Shaker Family of Sabbathday Lake, Maine. With the exception of track 15, all performances were recorded at the Shaker Village, Sabbathday Lake, Maine, on June and July, 2000, and were directed by Joel Cohen. Recording engineer was David Griesinger. Joel Cohen's research and editorial work on Shaker manuscripts has been supported in part by a grant from the Florence Gould Foundation.